Mastering Stage Hypnosis.

The Simple Guide To Entertaining With Hypnosis

Jesse Lewis

A few things you should know.

This book is self-written and self-published the grammar is horrible. The problem with creating a book that needs to be formatted as one talks, ie: hypnotic language, is that grammar during the inductions and such goes right out the window.

SO DON'T COMPLAIN, this is a book with hypnosis and hypnotic language. Run on sentences and confusion abound here! YOU HAVE BEEN WARNED!

If you want to have a professionally edited book go buy one. I will book a show instead!

The value in this book is worth its weight in gold so read it, its conversationally written, the value is also in the exercises so please do them as they will help you immensely.

Also you use any of the material in this book at your own risk. I hereby am stating do not do any of it as it can be dangerous in nature and I take no responsibility for any ones actions in regards to using the materials within. Be sensible and don't screw around and hurt people.

That is my disclaimer now I am un-sue-able besides I probably live in a different country than you so the joke is on you!

Now that that is over with I welcome you to the real book, let's ride!

Jesse Lewis

Stage Hypnosis –Jesse Lewis

Chapter 1: Intro and opportunity

Hello and welcome to this book all about stage hypnosis and the world of entertaining. I do not know why you have come to this book but you are in for a treat. If you are a brand new aspiring stage hypnotist I know you will find some useful stuff here. If you are an old pro that is long in the tooth well this book will challenge you to some new ideas and hopefully make your show better.

There is a huge opportunity for you to create the life you want using stage hypnosis if you are willing to work hard. There are many that have come before you that have used stage hypnosis to create the lives they want as well, I am one of them.

At this point you are probably wondering – Who the Hell is Jesse Lewis?

The simple answer is I am a father of two, a crazy husband and one damn great stage hypnotist! Talk about ego right!

Here is the family:

Well this is your first lesson and it is all about the true nature of hypnosis. Without ego, without confidence you simply will not be as good of a hypnotist as you can be. Confidence allows you to rule the stage and create an air of authority. So close your eyes take a deep breath and become confident right now. Open your eyes, wait a second you can't hear me...

There are many opportunities with stage hypnosis you could:

- Create a steady part or full time income
- Have a lot of fun traveling to and performing shows
- Meet a lot of people you never would have before
- Work on large and small stages everywhere
- Build the life you want

The opportunities are virtually endless, let me explain.

In the USA by itself there are about 40,000 high schools, limitless corporations, 1000's of associations, 10's of thousands of fairs and festivals, 1000;s of casinos, 1000's of colleges, 1000's of service clubs, resorts, bars, comedy clubs and those are only the markets that are on the surface, never mind all of the other opportunities to perform elsewhere. If a person really wanted to they could be performing every day of the week all year long and some do.

You don't live in the USA? Well neither do I. I live in Canada and the opportunities here are virtually the same. What about in Australia? The UK? France? Germany? Finland? Indonesia? Yes the opportunities are there as well. The only places I would suggest not becoming a stage hypnotist is in places where it is illegal! Don't do this stuff if it will get your head chopped off.

So what is stopping you? I would guess it is knowledge and fear. This book aims to give you knowledge and get rid of your fear.

One thing I need you to do before you go any further is to take any of those old beliefs or teachings about hypnosis you may have and throw them away! Yes right out the dam window, get rid of them! This is a brand new training manual for you so use it like you would a brand new training.

Wipe your mind of those preconceived notions about what hypnosis is and get ready for the wildest ride of your life. You see those old misconceptions of hypnosis will be tested and who knows maybe you agree or do not agree with me. I don't really care because the world and hypnosis has changed over time it will continue to do so as well. This manual might just be crap by the year 2050 who knows!

In the past hypnotists used what is called a progressive relaxation induction where they hypnotized people over a 20-40 minute span before the show even started. This led to really long and boring shows. These days however most stage hypnotists have dumped those old progressive relaxation inductions for more modern and faster methods like rapid and even instant inductions. This is a good direction for hypnosis to lead but also a bad one as a lot more people have started to believe hypnosis cannot be as simple as someone yelling sleep! It can be that simple with the right people and if you are confident.

I know you can become a stage hypnotist and that the opportunity is there for you too! Why? Because in 2007 I did my very first stage hypnosis show, six months later I was able to quit my job and do this full time. I have not stopped since!

This is a long way from where I began of course, growing up for me was not a great experience. I grew up on my grandfather's farm in Saskatchewan, we had no plumbing, power was supplied with an extension cord stung over a quarter mile of fence, we had no phone, my mother was on welfare and she was a hoarder of garbage. I don't tell you this so you can pity me, that is the last thing I want. I tell you this so you know where I am coming from. Those conditions left one thing in me growing up and that is the desire to succeed.

I want you to have that same desire that same passion that same drive and then you can know for certain you will succeed, because make no qualms about it, stage hypnosis is a business that you can make a living at. To make a good living it will take your drive and your passion to do so. As one of my first mentors said when I first started: The first person you hypnotise is yourself. Thanks for that motivation Geoff because I did hypnotize myself and damn if my life is not exactly what I wanted it to be back then!

Look at me mommy I am doing a big corporate show!

Chapter 2: The Truth about hypnosis

Opinions on hypnosis are as many as insects on earth:

There are many opinions of what hypnosis is and they are all as valid as the next, the simple truth is that science has yet to really define what hypnosis is at all. Even though some scientific studies show that while hypnotized a person experiences the suggestions as reality, a lot of people think hypnosis does not exist and you are not going to convince them, short of them experiencing it.

Even when they do experience it you probably will not convince them. They will say well I did not feel any different, I was awake the whole time, I could hear you, I was just playing along. These attitudes are all reflections of what they believe hypnosis is. Part of your job is to retrain them as to what to expect during the performance and while they are hypnotized.

A lot of people do think hypnosis does exist and may even be afraid of it. These people are not fools they just believe in some odd things. I bet you believe in weird things too like the Sasquatch or ghosts or hypnosis. I have been on both sides as a stage hypnotist believing and not believing because of my experiences. One of the biggest problems is that hypnosis is somewhat subjective depending on the level of hypnosis you have them in. So....

Who the hell cares as long as it works and you put on a show: That is my basic philosophy, I am primarily an entertainer these days and would have no problem going on stage and doing 60 minutes of entertainment with no volunteers. However 99 percent of stage hypnotists really could not do this at all because they have not trained themselves to be entertaining. We will take a look at basic showmanship in one of the future chapters but for now all you need to know is that you must be entertaining. Droning on – you are now getting sleepy- with a monotone voice will not cut it in todays entertainment world. You need pizazz, flair, and real entertainment value. It is all in this book so read and do the homework and you will be better that 80 percent of stage hypnotists out there that just drone on and on and on and on... oops I'm doing it right now!

My personal opinion on what hypnosis is is a very simple one: It is people following any suggestion the hypnotist gives, period. Ask them to move a certain way and they do – they are hypnotized! Ask them to scratch their nose and they do - they are hypnotized. Ask them to smell farts and they do – they are hypnotised.

How you achieve putting them into a hypnotic state (where they are compliant to you) really depends on you and your style. For me I prefer to use a classic stage hypnosis format for my shows which is what I will teach you throughout this book:

1. Introduction
2. Pre-talk
3. Pre-tests
4. Induction
5. Skits
6. Post hypnotics
7. Emerging

This is the most time tested format for a hypnosis show but in the final section I will give you some ideas that challenge this format. The world is a changing place and hypnosis is constantly changing with the fast pace that this entails. These days there is everything from séance style hypnosis to hypnosis with no actual hypnosis! Those old 45 minute progressive relaxation inductions are not a valid way to entertain any longer and people will walk out on them.

In todays contemporary world we must adapt our shows to what the audiences want. What do they want – entertainment, fun, drama, theater and a connection to the performance. That is what makes hypnosis truly great. There is nothing better than watching your friend, sister, mother, brother, become the star of the show and make no mistake your volunteers are truly the stars of the show.

The clinical definition of hypnosis is the bypass of the critical factor and establishment of acceptable selective thinking. This basically just means people following directions that are not offensive to them.

But wait: If that is the definition it means you could never get a person to do something against their morals right? Well that is true and not true at the same time. Morals are flexible… If you put a person in the right situation they would do almost anything. For instance would you shoot your friend in the foot for 1 million dollars? What would you do if someone attacked your family and you had the means to stop it? If you were to get a person in hypnosis to believe that this was actually happening you could theoretically get them to attack someone. In most stage hypnosis situations this is highly unlikely but if one of your preconceptions is that people will not do anything against their will then you are incorrect. People will not do anything against their circumstance is a better road to take.

The skills you learn in this book do give you great power and with that power does come great responsibility. So be responsible like Spiderman.

The final thing you need to understand before you move on in this book is something near and dear to me and to everyone who has ever mastered hypnosis. First off to master something takes time. All of the base hypnotic skills are here in this book but to truly master takes patience practice and perseverance. To truly become a master at anything you need to immerse yourself in it. To get down to the deep core of why, how, and when it works is essential to your journey. No book can ever teach you mastery but a good one can go a long way in helping you with the journey. So today it is time to make a powerful oath to yourself:

Another corporate show!

Repeat These Words

I will learn everything this book has to teach, I will become a true master of stage hypnosis, I am now becoming the best stage hypnotist I can be, I will use these skills responsibly and ethically to create the life I desire.

Let's get to hypnotizing!

Chapter 3: Your first hypnotic induction

Oh no it's scary, what if you fail or worse what if you make some ones head explode! What if you make them impotent! The likely hood of that is very slim. So let's just do this together!

- **Let's hypnotize someone!**

Hypnosis is getting a person to follow your directions, so for right now just find someone you can practice with and don't even mention hypnosis just tell them you want to try something. Ask them to place their hands right in front of them on their lap and breathe in and out deeply. Now ask them to think of something funny and if they want they can begin to smile. Ask them to allow themselves to intensify that funny thing and if they choose they can even let out a little giggle. By this point they should have at least smiled and if so you have elicited your very first hypnotic response!

YOU GAVE A SUGGESTION THEY FOLLOWED THAT IS ALL HYPNOSIS IS!

Oh but it is so small just a giggle or a smile. Well truthfully it is a door into bigger and better phenomenon. It is your job to build on this response and create something bigger.

So you want a "real" hypnotic induction now do you? Well grab that same person and continue along with this progressive relaxation and watch what they do. A big part of your job as a hypnotist is to be a master observer of your subjects so read this out loud to them and have conviction in your voice: (yes old pro's I am teaching the basics, first a progressive relaxation. It is the training wheels and don't worry later in the book we will master better techniques but for now do the work everyone)

Please just sit back and relax, allow yourself to breathe in naturally, and close your eyes. I would like you to imagine warmth somewhere inside you starting to grow, this warmth will begin to relax you and as you begin to relax you will find that you can allow your mind to follow each and every single suggestion I give from this point forward.

The mind is a wonderful thing anything you can imagine you can achieve and knowing this will allow you to begin to achieve bigger and better things. In fact as I read this that you can achieve almost anything your heart desires if you choose to allow yourself to achieve it.

Now is the time for your dreams to truly come true, I would like you to think of a cloud at the very top of your head and as this cloud is at the very top of your head making things kind of foggy first on your four head and then moving down to your eyes and into your brain making things foggy or an foggy or that gentle warmth creeps up and allows you to just relax in the fog can continue down over your shoulders through your neck relaxing as it goes each and every single muscle as you breathe out drifting now down through your chest and you might find out as it drifts your breathing gets a little bit deeper and it goes down to your stomach and your breathing relaxes even more and ensure back muscles and all the tension you have their can just melt away whenever you're ready and as it melts away you can relax even more and as that's cloud gently goes through your abdomen and hips allowing each and every muscle to relax you realize the deeper you go the better you feel and the better you feel the deeper you will go into this wonderful warm relaxation as your hips start to relax and down all through your legs every muscle nerve and fibre losing all the tension of the day allowing yourself to drift and float within this cloud allowing yourself to let that relaxation go down through your knee and fives through your cabs all the way down through your ankles letting that relaxation to flow within you to the very tips of your tongue. Like you to focus on your eyelids and just want you to relax was eyelids completely and totally completely and totally taken a steep breath in and just relax and let that relaxation to flow all the way out through the entire rest of your body in a huge wave through your whole body your arms your chest your legs your time all of just flowing a look away from your eyes relaxing you completely to the point where you just become like a wet dishcloth and in a few moments all lift up your hand drop back down in your lap and when I do just let that hand drop completely loose and limp relaxed as if you were a noodle or dishcloth just down right back into your lap.

-Lift hand and drop back down-

that's right allow that hand become completely loose limp and relaxed and as it does you can find yourself drifting deeper and deeper relaxed. In a few moments and ask you to just count and outwards from 10 with each number I want you say the words deeper relaxed so to go like this 10 deeper relaxed nine deeper relaxed and you'll find that when you get to one you be so relaxed feeling so good going so confident about yourself that you just open your eyes and when you come out of this relaxed state on the last final number one your entire day will just be completely stress-free and relaxed and that you can come back to this state any time you want to relax just by doing that 10 count 10 deeper relaxed nine deeper relaxed so let's begin with you start your count and when you get to one you just don't your eyes going completely loose limp and relaxed let's go.

-From here you let them count themselves up out of hypnosis and have also given them the gift of relaxation-

What a run on sentence! But you can see the first beginnings of hypnotic language right there, the words "and as" are a very powerful way to link things together and cause further hypnotic phenomenon.

But have you achieved anything? Well you gave them a gift and you observed them and what hypnosis looks like for that person. Every person is a little bit different and will act differently. You will find as you progress through this book that you can and will be able to spot different things that are unique to each of your volunteers.

The induction you just read is a progressive relaxation and actually way too long for my personal tastes because it would take from 8-12 minutes to perform on stage. By that point I like to be into my first skit already! Generally my induction is 3-5 minutes and pre-talk is about 5 this means I am actually getting skits started by the 10 minute mark of most of my shows. Some hypnotists even the big ones in Vegas don't start the skits until the 30-45 minute mark. That is way too much wasted time for me.

When you perform it will be up to you to develop your own style of performance but it is a good idea to follow a format that is worked for a long time like the one that is outlined in the showmanship part of this book. Now that you've officially put someone into hypnosis and now understand how easy it is you are ready to understand the most important part of the show the pre-talk!

Me performing the pre-talk suggestibility tests or pre-tests with a lovely volunteer!

Chapter 4: The Pre-talk

This is where the real hypnosis happens. Without a good pre-talk to you, you will be left in the dust with no volunteers no show and no pay check.

A good pre-talk really is the difference between a fantastic show and a piece of crap show. Every Pre talk is different and you need to develop your own. The tools in this following chapter will help you create a pre-talk that follows a formula that is time tested but is still your own with your own personality.

This section is your guide to creating a powerful pre-talk!

This section is broken down into several modules that are going to teach you the easiest step by step process of doing a pre-talk that is engaging, entertaining and establishes you as the expert entertainer on the stage.

On top of that it is going to be fun! Why a section on doing pre-talks? Because it is needed! Too many hypnotists are using stock Pre-talks and not making them their own! This diminishes the art and craft of hypnosis. Others are giving bad pre-talks and are not being entertaining while they do! With a really good pre-talk the chances of an awesomely successful show go way up. Now is the time for you to develop a great pre-talk that is entertaining engaging and educational. So let's get right into it!

The 3 E's are the foundation of any good pre-talk

- Establish yourself as an expert performer/hypnotist
- Entertain the audience with the pre-talk
- Engage them on the level they need to be engaged on

Establish yourself as an expert performer/hypnotist

It is important that at some point during the pre-talk you establish your credibility with the audience. This makes them feel comfortable knowing that you will not make their heads explode. It can be very simple or very complex

Entertain the audience

This is where you actually give them something to think about jokes, drama, creating expectation of what is going to happen this is all part of entertaining them

Engage them with what they need

This really comes down to knowing what type of audience you have and giving them what they need to be the best subjects.

One rule to remember is that the audience just like your volunteers give continual feedback throughout the show.

Without the 3 E's

Your pre-talk will not be strong and you may have a bad show.

This section is going to be split into several parts that go into detail about how to achieve the 3 E's and have a great pre-talk that you can change and suit to any audience. Let's get started into section one!

Pre-talk Primer Module One

The framework

A Pre-talk is based on three things

- The Crowd type!
- The feel of the crowd!
- And your ability to read the crowd and what they need!

So for different crowds you will base your pre-talk on different things. Let's start with the general basics of a standard scripted pre-talk

BUT BEFORE THAT

GET YOURSELF PUMPED UP BEFORE THE PRETALK

Yes pumped up, the audience reacts to what they see on stage so bring out some energy when you come out!

Workbook time: HOMEWORK THAT YOU MAY HATE: watch the next episode of wrestling, you see be WWE specific, Study the entrances which ones excite you, which ones are boring? Why? Answer the questions below in the book!

Are they engaging and why?

Does one stand out?

What is good about them?

What would you do to improve them?

How long are they?

Are there other places you can go to watch live entrances, if so list them and study them!

Are there other shows you can watch that are for a live crowd? If so go see their entrances and critique them. Then figure out your entrance! Make it engage the audience!

Basic Pre-talk Framework

1. Engage the audience right at the start
2. Talk about myths or fears
3. Explain they have been in hypnosis before
4. Rules of who you want
5. Reasons to volunteer for show
6. BOR pitch
7. Get the audience to participate (pre-test or gag with whole audience)
8. Call for volunteers
9. OPTIONAL TEACH THEM HOW TO RESPOND TO A LIVE SHOW!

That is a lot of basics and many of the pieces are actually optional for many audiences! It is up to you to read the audience! Let's go over each in a little more detail!

1. Engage the audience!

In this step it is your chance to shine. It is the first time you step onto the stage in front of your audience. It is time to make an impact. There are several options to accomplish this! Let's talk about engaging the audience.

Definition: Engage 1. occupy, attract, or involve (someone's interest or attention). 2. participate or become involved in.

So what can we do to engage an audience?

Tools for engaging the audience:

YOUR Introduction:

You should have a custom recorded introduction for the group type write it out and get it professionally recorded on Fiverr for five bucks it is cheap and easy and you should have five bucks. If not sell something and go get a damn introduction made.

Your walk on:

Do you walk on all sad and dejected? How you introduce yourself is how people will see you! Do you have confidence in your skills? If nothing else smile and walk out like you are superman because hell yes you are a hypnosis god!

Get them to Laugh and build trust in you:

Laughter is a great equalizer we all love to laugh so let's bring out your comedic talents and get a joke going.

Make them do something:

Yep get them involved right away! This is a really easy way to engage them. Getting them to yell something at you to focus their attention or participate in a chant. "When I say ___ you say ____" is always a great way to get them engaged!

How you move is important!

Think about how pro wrestlers come out instantly you know the person is there to perform a show and it takes you by the cajones into the show! It does not have to be a flashy show but should establish what is going to happen and what is expected!

This is your time to open and is your first chance to introduce yourself so make an impact!

Examples of these things in action:

Pre music programing, pump them up appropriately

Audience pump ups: Clapping, Woooo, Drum roll, when I say ___
you say ___! Scream a word of your choosing! BOUNCE BOUNCE!

WORKBOOK:

Write down three (different than the examples) pump ups that you
can use in your pre-talks!

1.

2.

3.

2. Talk about myths and fears

This is designed to first dispel myths that are out there and to get rid
of reasons people have to not volunteer! It also establishes your
credibility as the expert hypnotist you are!

You do not need to tackle the myths much with crowds in certain
markets like schools or grads but with corporate and service clubs it
is best to include this in your pre-talk!

Some common myths you can explain

- Hypnosis is not sleep
- In hypnosis they will not act like a zombie
- They will not tell their deepest secrets
- They cannot get stuck in hypnosis

When you dispel myths you need to add in some jokes related to the myth for instance with the acting like a zombie I often pretend I am a zombie, it is good for a laugh and does the job!

You need to put your own personality into it!

WORKBOOK: List 10 more myths about hypnosis that you can have in your pre-talk (you will never use all of them unless you give a speech on hypnosis to gain business)

1.

2.

3.

4.

5.

6.

7.

8.

9.

10.

3. Explain everyone has been in hypnosis before

Every person on earth has been in hypnosis before, it's your job to let your audience know this is true and hypnosis is a natural process! They do not have to be afraid since they have actually experienced it many times. This is a chance for some comedy as well! Can you think of something funny to say about any of the times that people go into hypnosis in their daily lives?

Hypnosis in daily life examples:

Driving and lose time

Keys being where they were all along and the subject knew they were there when they were lost(negative hallucination)

We go into hypnosis just before bed and just before we wake up we go into hypnosis

Reading, watching TV, listening to music, when you just get sucked into it and forget about the world that is a state of hypnosis.

Workbook: List 3 more examples of times people go into hypnosis in their daily life.

    1.

    2.

    3.

4. Rules of who you want to volunteer and how they can do it!

Every hypnotist has rules of who can and who cannot volunteer! I suggest you be firm with this and make a joke out of it at the same time. My joke is at the end " and there is only one other type of person who is not allowed to come on my stage, That type of person is someone who is completely crazy, please don't come up! You know who you are"

I also do not let pregnant women come up as I do not need to have a baby on my stage (at least a real one) everyone else is welcome on my stage provided they are able to get up there. If they are not (in a wheelchair or otherwise disabled) they can still be in the show but not actually on my stage. In those circumstances I generally put them in front of the stage as it is one hell of a lot safer. There is a video out there somewhere of a hypnotized person in a wheel chair wheeling themselves off the stage and messing themselves up pretty bad. Be smart be safe.

So what are your rules?

Types of rules:

1. People that cannot volunteer?

2. How they are allowed to come on stage

3. How they are to sit

4. You can address all of this quickly and with some fun as well!

Workbook: write down your rules for your pre-talk!

YOUR RULES :

1.

2.

3.

4.

5.

5. Reasons to volunteer

At this point I like to give them reasons to volunteer and go into hypnosis. For me my reasons include:

- It makes them feel great
- They will have more fun
- They will feel as if they have slept 8 hours in the span of the show
- They will be the stars of the night
- It gets rid of stress
- They can blame me for the silly things they do

What will they get from your show when they volunteer? Is it just fun, will it relieve stress, will it change their lives. This is all very important stuff and leads into the next section

Workbook time:

What 3 reasons and benefits can you give to volunteer that you can actually deliver during the show?

1.

2.

3.

6. BOR PITCH

Once you establish the benefits of hypnosis you can pitch your recorded products quickly by simply stating, *"For those interested in the therapeutic side of hypnosis I will have CD's available for sale right over at that table after the show."*

7. Get the audience to participate

Getting the audience to participate will help improve your show! The more involved the audience in the experience of your show the better. During the pre-talk is a great time to establish that this is an audience participation show! Without the participation of the audience you really do not have a show to start with so get them involved. This can be a full audience pre-test or a gag, it is up to you.

Getting the audience to participate:

This is not for every audience but works well for most. Call for a single volunteer and do a Pre-test or a gag with them and the audience. This is designed to be fun and not embarrassing! Kind of a big old hey we are here to have fun so let's have fun. If you plan on doing a gag do it first to break the ice and then do a follow up pre-test to prove you are the expert.

My favourite gag currently is to get them to hold out their hands like they will be doing magnetic hands (covered later) and get them all to clench their fists and move them up and down alternating. Then say "If any of you were worried about being embarrassed you should not be because right now you are all milking fake cows!" Despite the way it reads on paper when delivered correctly it gets a good laugh. I move on from that into either the magnetic hands or magnetic fingers pre-test with the whole audience.

Explain the show is all about fun audience participation and not going to be embarrassing and move on into a pre-test!

What possible gags could you do?

Yes it is workbook time again

Workbook: think up three possible gags that you may be able to use in your pre-talk!

    1.

    2.

    3.

Possible Pre-tests

After I do the gag I generally do a pre-test with the whole audience. In a future chapter we will be taking a look at over 20 pre-tests you can use during your show in detail and how you can use a simple pre-test to do a full blown induction. This is how most instant inductions are handled and if you choose I will go over the skills needed to do this.

8. Call for volunteers

Your call for volunteers is crucial there are a few things you should do to achieve maximum success in getting volunteers!

Create anticipation "In a moment I will call for volunteers, when I do the chairs will fill up and we will have a lot of fun. I expect all of these chairs to fill up fast so if you want a spot get up here when I say to come up" This lets them know the call to action is coming and they will only have a limited time to get up there and volunteer.

Let them know they will be the stars of the show! "The people that come up will be the stars of the show so on the count of three come up and volunteer"

Get audience to applaud those that come up "Everyone clap as the volunteers come up and fill these chairs let's get this show going. 123 they are the stars of the show"

Get out of the way and give people room to come up! Play an upbeat song as the volunteers come on up! If you are having trouble getting volunteers let them know a few more benefits of coming up!

OPTIONAL STEP LETTING THEM KNOW HOW TO RESPOND TO LIVE ENTERTAINMENT

Have you ever gone to a live show and the show was stellar but the audience sucked? Want to know the reason? We sit in front of a box for eight hours per day and don't clap, don't laugh and most of all don't interact!

Being a good audience member is becoming a lost art. As entertainers we actually have to start to teach our audience how to react. During my pre-talk I add one simple line that makes all of the difference. I get them to put their hands up and ask: now everyone if you like the show what are you going to do? They inevitably clap. I then say now if you think it's funny what are you going to do? They laugh. It is a little thing but it works to get them to know they are not bumps on a log and can interact with the show.

Not all audiences need a full pre-talk

The components that I have shown here are really a base guideline and can be changed out to use as needed. The important part is that you suit your pre-talk to the audience and their needs. Some audiences you will not be able to sell BOR for others don't need to know about the myths. It is up to you to really gage your audience and don't worry about making a mistake no one knows about it but you!

One other thing! It is up to you to create your pre-talk! You have to do the work actually use it so it has to suit you! If you are uncomfortable saying or using something I describe just don't do it! Your show is YOUR show. So make it the best it can be! Holy crap that is a lot of information!

In the next section we break down using hypnotic language to make your pre-talk more effective in bringing people on stage!

Your Pre-talk and Hypnotic Language

Hypnotic language in the Pre-talk

It is important to understand the basics of hypnotic language in your pre-talk so you can have more success bringing people up on stage and preparing them for hypnosis. Hypnotic language does not have to be hard. Some trainers make this way too complicated, the secret is to talk normally with emphasis on certain things!

Let's start with a basic hypnotic language tool the presupposition!

Presuppositions

This is where you presuppose an event or outcome before it happens for instance: "In a moment I will call for volunteers and *you will come up here* and fill the stage!" This presupposes that people will come up and volunteer. Simple right!

Another: "*When you experience hypnosis* you lose all of your stress and feel good." This statement does not give them a choice it presupposes with the word "when" and states directly that they will go into hypnosis!

Can you create some presuppositions for your show? Good phrases to use are time modifiers: When, tonight, before, as,

First find the presuppositions in the following sentences this will help you create your own later:

When you allow yourself to let go tonight hypnosis will come easily to you!

Ladies and gentlemen tonight's show will be a lot of fun when you let go of all of your stress.

Ladies and gentlemen in a moment I will hypnotize you to have fun and then you will let go into a deep state of hypnosis!

When you are hypnotized you will follow my direction faster and easier than you ever thought possible

When you perform hypnosis it is important that you now understand presuppositions!

WORKBOOK: Now write out some presuppositions for yourself and your pre-talk!

1.

2.

3.

These are also great for when doing the hypnotic inductions as they can actually "force" people into hypnosis subconsciously by presupposing the next step in the hypnotic process!

This brings us to EMBEDED Commands! The presuppositions were full of them could you tell? They are an integral part of getting people to follow you and volunteer!

An embedded command is a command that is hidden within seemingly normal speech. For a masters course on how to use these just watch your favourite political speech and you will see them used everywhere in it.

Let's look at a presupposition from before and see if you can find the embedded commands:

Find the embedded commands

Ladies and gentlemen in a moment I will hypnotize you to have fun and then you will let go into a deep state of hypnosis!

Embedded Commands and Presuppositions!

When you perform hypnosis it is important that you now understand presuppositions! So in the last sentence there is one of each can you tell what they are?

When you perform hypnosis is the presupposition

You will now understand is the embedded command.

Make some of your own embedded commands

Workbook: Write down 5 embedded commands and presuppositions that you can use in your normal pre-talk speech

1.
2.
3.
4.
5.

Practice saying each as this will help you get used to them for your pre-talk.

Embedded commands should have a slight emphasis on the command while presuppositions require no extra technique

Example: When you perform hypnosis it is important that "you now understand" presuppositions! When you get hypnotized you will be fully awake and aware "you will follow directions" and have a lot of fun.

The simplest way for me to create an embedded command is to talk a little bit like Captain Kirk (original star trek) and point out certain parts of your speech. Like him or hate him, President Obama is a master of the embedded command. Study him if you want to become a master too.

Pacing and Leading!

Pacing and leading is all about getting the audience into the "yes" set, this is the theory that if you can get a person to say yes repeatedly they will continue to follow the path of least resistance and continue saying yes to anything that is even remotely suitable. Car salesmen are the masters of this and you should be too!

For example: Welcome ladies and gentlemen tonight we are here for a hypnosis show. I am Jesse Lewis and I will be your performer tonight. It is going to be a lot of fun!

PACE, PACE, LEAD! Their brain goes True –> True -> Must be true

Pace

Welcome ladies and gentlemen tonight we are here for a hypnosis show.

Pace

I am Jesse Lewis and I will be your performer tonight.

Lead

It is going to be a lot of fun!

We follow the path of least resistance sub-consciously by creating the yes set! Now it is time for you to create pacing statements

Workbook: Create five true statements about any event.

Pacing statements:

1.
2.
3.
4.
5.

Now create 3 leading statements

1.
2.
3.
4.

This is hard work but it is worth it! It will make you a better hypnotist to know these tools and put them to use

The next part of the pre-talk is your body language

Body language is important to your pre-talk sequence. You have to have confidence in yourself or no one else will. You have to be pumped up or the audience simply will not trust you and not be pumped up either! You have to be professional for that audience and create a real show!

Body language basics:

Your hygiene

Are you gross? Do you have greasy hair? Halitosis from hell? Dirty chewed on fingernails? All of these play a factor into how the audience perceives you and JUDGES YOU! If you have bad hygiene you will not be perceived as professional! This is not a course on good hygiene but make sure you are as presentable as possible.

Your dress deserves as much attention as your hygiene

Yep, no matter what venue you perform in you need to dress appropriately for that audience. For bars it may be fine to wear a T-shirt and jeans but for corporate that just will not fly! So dress appropriately and wear at least one level above your intended audience.

For bars, A nice shirt and clean pants may be enough, for schools dress like a teacher would, for corporates it depends on the event some are black shirt and tie and others are full tuxedo. For those events I suggest asking what the dress code is and dressing appropriately!

Actual body language (your movements)

There are many ways to show confidence without being a jerk about it, let's get into them now!

Displaying confidence what not to do

- Get your hands out of your pockets, it looks dirty
- Fidgeting

- Do not cross your arms
- Bad posture
- Eyes downcast
- No Energy
- Shaking and fear

All of these things are part of your body language and each one is a display of poor confidence in yourself. It is your job to show confidence in yourself and your abilities. So at least play the part, displaying fake confidence is fine until you have it!

How to display confidence:

- Eyes forward and direct
- Stand up straight, shoulders back
- Have wide steps
- Smile Smile Smile
- Laugh

Use their own body language against them!

Sometimes in the audience you will catch someone with their arms crossed it means they are uncomfortable and worried about the situation! During the pre-talk I will often point that person out and actually ask the whole audience to uncross their arms and just put their hands on their lap. By forcing them to do this it sends an unconscious signal to them to let go and relax.

Your movement

Your movement on stage is important, often that is where your audience is directed and you can use that! Every movement you have on stage should have a purpose. If you want to display high energy have high energy movements. If you want to be more dramatic, slow down. If you want to be funnier embellish your movements to a point.

Most performers I know make huge mistakes with their body language by pacing and being fearful, me included. One way I have prevented myself from pacing the stage is to put a small piece of tape on the back of the volunteer's chairs to remind me to stop pacing. When you move on stage you are the star of the show. People naturally follow movement and it is your volunteers that are the true stars so let them be and take nothing away from them by pacing the stage. Ground yourself and stand that ground unless you absolutely need to move.

When you are critiquing your show in the future remember to come back to this section and read again about body language.

Creating that pre-talk

Pre-talk Framework

Pre show programing music
1. Engage the audience right at the start
2. Talk about myths or fears
3. Explain they have been in hypnosis before
4. Rules of who you want
5. Reasons to volunteer for show
6. BOR pitch
7. Get the audience to participate (pre-test or gag with whole audience)
8. Call for volunteers

Let's take a look at my intro and pre-talk!

Pre show -Upbeat appropriate music is playing

Jesse Lewis Audience Introduction hits, I jump up and down to get pumped, the introduction ends:

Sample pre-talk:

1. Engage the audience

I walk out on stage with arms open and am smiling

"Hello Ladies and Gentlemen. My name is Jesse Lewis and tonight I will be hypnotizing you! Tonight we are here to experience hypnosis but before we do that, it is important to understand the truth about hypnosis.

2. Talk about myths and fears

Lots of people are worried about hypnosis because there are a lot of myths about it. For instance some people think hypnosis is sleep but it really is not! When you get hypnotized you will be fully awake and aware and you will follow my directions and have a lot of fun. Some people worry they will tell their deepest darkest secrets but rest assured that simply does not happen. In fact you would never do anything in hypnosis that is against your morals. Of course if you have no morals then that is not my fault!

By the way some people worry about getting stuck in hypnosis, well that cannot happen, it is a natural state, so even if I died on stage you would come out of hypnosis within about a minute and see what was going on!

3. They have been in hypnosis before

You have been in hypnosis 1000's of times for instance, just before you go to sleep and just before you wake up you are in a hypnotic state, or when you are driving and lose focus for a few minutes and cannot remember driving that distance! That is all hypnosis.

4. Rules

There are a few rules to coming up. You must be willing to be hypnotized. You must be physically able to come on stage. The only other type of people I don't want are crazy people - you know who you are!

5. Reasons to volunteer

Many people wonder why they should volunteer. Well hypnosis reduces stress and in the course of the show you will feel as if you slept for eight hours straight! On top of that, during the show there are several motivational messages throughout that you can use to change anything that you want in your life!

6. (BOR) For those interested

I will have motivational hypnosis CD's available after the show for purchase right over there at that table!

7. Participate:

Before I call for volunteers I need just one person to come up here and stand with me! Awesome! Young man what is your name? ohh that's an awesome name for a lady! Now take your hands put them out in front of you and clench the fists. Awesome, everyone in the audience please do the same! Cool now move them up and down like this (milking cows). Now stop, if you were worried about being embarrassed, don't worry because you all look silly because you are milking cows!

That's right tonight's show is about audience participation! Without you there is no show so before we begin I want to show you exactly what hypnosis feels like. Put your hands out in front of you; don't worry no milking cows this time. Clasp them together palms flat, Point your index fingers out like this, Pull them apart and look at them. Ma'am, stop looking at me I am ugly look at your fingers. Now imagine a rubber band pulling them closer. Squeeze those palms together; imagine that rubber band getting stronger 1-2-3. Stop. For those that concentrated this worked great for those that did not that is fine too. That is exactly how hypnosis feels just like you feel now! In a moment I will call for volunteers, when I do, audience, you need to explode with applause to get them up here on the count of three you will volunteer 1-2-3.

Upbeat music!

That is my standard pre-talk suitable for almost everyone!

Now it is up to you to create yours; workbook time!

Full Blown Pre-talk exercise 1

Your introduction

How are you going to come out! Describe your ideal way to come out and introduce yourself to the audience.

This is all about being you, would there be flashing lights, would it be mellow and mysterious?

What music plays before your introduction hits?

What is the feel? Describe it in detail!

Exercise 2: Pacing statements

What are three pacing statements you can use during you Pre-talk

Remember a pacing statement is an absolutely true statement that leads into a leading statement

1.
2.
3.

Exercise 3

Leading statements

What are three leading statements you can use in your pre-talk?

1.
2.
3.

Exercise 4

From here you will write your pre-talk from the very beginning. Be detailed and write as if you are speaking to the audience! You will read it later to get it into your brain and then practice as well!

1. How you will introduce yourself to the audience and initially engage them: What will you say? (include hypnotic language)

Describe your body language:

2. Talk about myths and fears: What myths do you want to address?

Do you have a joke for that myth?

Describe your body language:

3. Explain when they have been in hypnosis before: When have they been in hypnosis before?

Do you have a joke to add here? What is it?

What is your body language?

4. Rules of who you want and don't want and stage safety rules: What are your rules?

What is your body language?

5. Reasons to volunteer for your show?

What are the reasons they should volunteer?

What is your Body language?

    6. BOR pitch: What is for sale? Where is it?

    7. Audience participation: Do you have a gag for this or not?

What is your pre-test:

Body language?

    8. Call for volunteers: What will you say?

What will you do to get maximum impact and volunteers from this?

What is your body language?

HOME WORK: Now it is time to practice

Read it word for word off of the page 5 times and grab a video camera and do it live without the script record it 5 more times! Review, look at your body language! Are you owning it?

Does it look polished? If not do it again and again. This is the path to mastery; get few index cards and write down on different cards– conservative corporate, school, grad, service club, comedy club, bar, corporate holiday party and any other type of venue or audience you can think of. Take those cards shuffle them and grab the top one then do a pre-talk for that specific audience starting from your introduction.

While you watch the recordings do you follow the script closely or is it spontaneous? If it is spontaneous, good but it should also look like you have done it 10000 times and have no fear! Think of it this way, you will practice 90 times for your very first performance and then you will have no fear. Do your pre talk in the car, do it in the shower, do it while making love. Hmm what was that! Don't do it while making love your partner will be angry trust me… stay away from inductions too…..

Review it! Review, look at your body language! Are you owning it! Does it look polished while you watch the recordings do you follow the script closely or is it spontaneous? When you are done this exercise do it 10 more times to practice and refine it. Until you feel ready then do it 10 more times to make sure it fits you! This may take a long time but because this is the most important part of the show it is worth it!

Pre-talk Advanced techniques

Hecklers, Attention Grabbers, Alpha Presence

It does not happen often but sometimes you will get hecklers at your shows. Your job is to be a pro and since you do not know who the heckler is you should be polite but dominant in handling them.

There are two basic ways to handle a heckler

1. Ignore them

Yes that is right ignore them!

When you ignore them they lose their power and make no mistake that is what they are trying to display. When you ignore them it sends a subtle message that they are beneath you and not even worth your time.

2. Acknowledge them

Acknowledge them and they gain power over you but it also allows you to put them in their place or more specifically the audience to put them in their place.

The specific line I use is "ladies and gentlemen I am sorry that this person is choosing to ruin tonight's event". Usually the heckler is actually a bully and the best way to deal with an adult bully is to punch them in the face! Unfortunately you cannot so let the audience handle the A-hole! When this does not work (rarely) I will actually stop the show and not continue until the heckler is dealt with. You must be very careful as this can backfire if the heckler is a person of importance in the group like a CEO or Manager. However it is also your job to make the show happen so make it happen no matter what.

Getting an audience's attention

Sometimes you will have an audience that just does not want to pay attention there are ways to handle this. Getting louder and louder is a simple way to draw attention and can get you on your way however it is also a way for you to be seen as the bad guy. Getting quieter and make those paying attention shush the others is a way to get the audience to do your dirty work for you.

The final option, and the worst in my opinion as it makes you into a diva, is to stop the show and wait for people to shut up while having a banter with the people who are listening mentioning every once in a while that you can wait as long as it takes for people to quiet down. Much of this can actually be prevented by establishing the alpha presence in the room. The simplest way to command a crowd is with the alpha presence, that is what the body language module is all about so get that damn intro ready and before you walk out blast it so people pay attention then- walk on with confidence and talk with confidence. This will help you not only on stage but in life too. People respect confident people so command respect. Be confident not cocky!

Practice this until it becomes natural and you will feel natural doing it. Don't be a dick, be dominant! The real secret is confidence and going out there and just doing it. One show is not your whole career so go out there and fail a few times like I did. Soon enough you will have that pre-talk down and be amazing with your stage hypnosis show. You will learn more from a fail than a great show and when you fail enough you get better and better.

Hypnotic headshot anyone? Dam I Am Pretty!

Chapter 5: More Hypnotic tools

Building rapport with you audience is essential which is what the pre-talk was all about but there are some advanced hypnotic tools you can use as well. Two of the most important tools in your arsenal are mirroring and matching. This is the process of pacing movements and eventually leading them in the direction you want.

Mirroring and matching

Here is how it works, they move their leg, you move your leg. They move their arm, you move your arm, they blink, you blink. All of this is done without their conscious knowledge and it creates a slight bond with them.

The most common form of mirroring during a hypnosis show is getting them to take a deep breath and doing the same thing at the same time. This creates a bond with your volunteers almost instantly doing this with your audience during the pre-talk can also increase volunteers coming up on stage. It is kind of pre hypnotizing them to come up.

Cross matching

There is another way to mirror and that is to cross match by mirroring their actions and moving a cross matching body part. They move their left leg you move your right, they scratch their head on the left you do it on the right. This can still create a powerful bond with your subjects.

PRACTICE TIME:

Go to your favourite restaurant and order a meal, sit there mirroring and matching people. The waiter or waitress, the fellow patrons, mirror movements, breathing, mannerisms, all of it. Do not get caught doing it though that is the secret, to keep it secret!

Earlier I talked about pacing and leading and how to pace with true statements which is a good way to get group compliance? This can also be used with things that are happening to individuals to gain their compliance by using the things they are experiencing to pace and then lead. This all ties into the signs of hypnosis.

When a person starts to experience the signs of hypnosis you simply pace them for instance:

Some of you may find that you need to swallow and this causes _____

Many of you may notice your eyes moving rapidly under your eyelids and this causes _____

Some of you may notice your face relaxing and as it does you _____

You may find your thoughts drifting and this causes you to _____

There are many signs of hypnosis and they can all be used with the pacing tool. So now it is time for you to create your own pacing and leading statements for the things you may soon be noticing in your volunteers.

Create a pacing statement for each of the following

1. Catalepsy
2. Dry throat
3. REM (EYE TWITCHING DURING SLEEP)
4. Relaxation
5. Crying (tear ducts let go as they relax)
6. Placid muscles
7. Extreme focus
8. Confusion
9. Heating up

This is basically using hypnotic phenomenon to induce more hypnotic phenomenon. It is a wonderful way to get compliance.

Looping: is another tool that should be in your tool belt here is a basic loop "the more you relax the deeper you go and the deeper you go the more you relax. " This creates an endless loop of relaxation.

There are other suggestions you can give such as, the deeper you go the better you feel and the better you feel the deeper you go. These are great little sentences that can deepen the hypnotic state and get further compliance.

Anchoring

Another tool you can use is anchoring. Anchoring is the process of giving a suggestion that whenever something happens another reaction will happen. You will be using anchors repeatedly through your show for instance "when I say sleep now our head will fall forward and you will relax completely closing your eyes." Or any time you count and a person does something at the end is an anchor. You can use this to deepen trance as well for instance "each and every breath takes you ten times deeper from this point forward." This effectively anchors a person's breathing (something they cannot stop) into putting them into hypnosis.

Chapter 6: Pre-test mania

All about hypnotic pre-tests

In the pre-talk portion of this book we had talked briefly about hypnotic pre-tests and how to use them effectively. This section is going to go down the road of teaching you various pre-tests that I find work well on stage. Every one of these can be turned into an instant induction if you so choose. It is my personal theories that once a person follows some basic pre-tests you are ready to put them under and go on with the show. This is especially true with younger volunteers in schools and even colleges.

If you own my previous work on the subject of pre-tests called the pre-test progression you will know that this is really an excerpt from that work. I also have a full video course available for purchase on pre-tests at showbizsuccesssecrets.com in the store section.

How to do these tests

Simply put you can do most of these tests right off the bat or you can alter them to suit your needs. I use them during my pre-talk or as instant proof of hypnosis in everyday life. Most are fool proof and work really well as long as you are confident that they will work.

I suggest you do one or two easy ones with the whole audience during your pre-talk. Make sure they are safe and people will not hurt themselves in the audience.

One last note on how to perform all of these effects with hypnosis.

Some of the effects will require you to be a keen observer of what is going on with your subject and to feed those observations back to them. For instance, the stuck hand and real stuck foot both require you to feed back the persons experience to them.

If you do not feed it back it may not be the end of the world and the effect still may work but to become a truly great hypnotist you must be always watching always seeing always feeling what your subjects are going through, what they are feeling.

One exercise I like to do is to watch people discreetly in public places and mirror their actions building rapport with them until they actually start to mirror me. It can take some practice but this is easily done.

Creating a loop is simple you can just say 'that's right and the more that happens the more _____ your _____ becomes more and more.

A common one most hypnotists use is the more you relax the deeper you go and the deeper you go the better you feel causing you to become more relaxed. It is a loop that feeds itself in the subconscious mind and can truly make a person have that hypnotic experience.

Last but defiantly not least

This is not the end of your learning if you are just a beginner. In fact there is so much more to learn that this work could not encompass it all so expect further works in the future. I have been watching the street hypnosis scene from afar for a long time and have been performing stage hypnosis for even longer. The one thing every one fails to mention about street hypnosis is that half the time it is just Pre-tests which is what this section is all about.

For the skilled hypnotist you already know how to turn people into those instant hypnotic subjects that you love for those not so experienced look.

Here is a list of the tests you will learn in this section.

1. Light and heavy hands
2. Magnetic hands
3. Body part movement test

4. Laughter Test
5. Pen Lock
6. Impossible to get up from floor
7. Unable to bend leg
8. Stuck hand
9. Basic name amnesia
10. Fingertip sticking
11. Fingertips will not touch
12. Missing Number
13. And a whack of other ones too!

Each test will be featured on its own page and one thing you must remember is this book is about entertaining others with y=hypnosis not just yourself, so go out and practice these pretests on anyone that will allow it. Make it as entertaining as possible and get those performance chops up to snuff!

Light and heavy hands

This is a classic test that dates back a long time. I first learned it from Ormund Mcgills Encyclopaedia of Stage Hypnotism and I use it all the time during stage shows as a convincer.

Effect: Light and Heavy Hands

The hypnotist asks the subject to put one hand palm facing up towards the roof and one hand palm facing down with the subjects arms stretched in front of them. One arm raises other arm lowers at the suggestions of the hypnotist.

How to: Light and Heavy Hands

Ask the subject to place arms outstretched and put the right hand palm downward and the left arm palm upwards.

Remind them to be steady if they are standing or sitting and ask them to close their eyes. This is to prevent them from falling over and hurting themselves.

Ask them to imagine something heavy in the hand with the palm facing upwards that gets heavier and heavier the higher you count. (a rock, a pail of sand, or water, or a book are good examples of heavy things.)

Attached the other hand the one with the palm facing downward is a string that goes up into the air to a balloon or kite and it is rising higher and higher as that arm gets lighter and lighter with every number you count upwards. Jerking in the wind pulling higher and higher.

One the stone gets heavier.

Two that balloon gets lighter and lighter .

Three that balloon gets so light rising up now higher and higher.

Continue to make suggestions of palm upward hand getting heavier and palm downward hand getting lighter.

Remember to use imagery with your suggestions like: Buckets of water, sand, Cement, Balloons, Kites. The more imagery you use with any hypnotic pre-test the better it will work.

Some people will mess with you and purposely not let it work,

I have one word for them NEXT. It is impossible to do these or any hypnotic technique without having a willing volunteer.

The fact is some people are idiots and after much deliberation with the universe I came to the conclusion this wonderful world will get them in the end. The technique does not fail the, the subjects do, so let it slide off your back and know you are on your way to becoming a better hypnotist.

Magnetic hands

This is yet an old classic of hypnotism and indeed it relies on human body functions as much as genuine hypnosis it can be a hugely effective opener and works well both as a single person demonstration and for groups.

Effect

A person's hands come together as if compelled by magnets or an elastic band.

How To

Ask the spectator to place arms straight out in front of them with palms facing each other.

Get them to place hands about shoulder width apart. Make sure they are stable and know to catch themselves if they begin to fall.

Ask them to close their eyes and imagine magnets or a rubber band pulling their hands together.

Repeat it a few times while talking about what is happening to them. As you stand there your hands stretched in front of you allowing yourself to follow directions quicker and easier than you ever imagined your hands are compelled as if by magnets or an elastic band to come closer and closer together.

This is an automatic body response like magnetic finger and it is almost impossible for it to fail unless the subject is being an idiot and not following directions.

Body part action test

This test is really more about confidence than anything else.

It is simply causing a person's body to either move unexpectedly or to force them to notice something that is going on in their body that they may not have noticed before.

It truly is hypnosis in my belief and is extremely effective.

Effect

The hypnotist causes a person's body part to move or twitch.

How to

Option one: Stand a person up straight.

Get them to imagine a force from your hand to the part you want to move. Ask them to make that part heavy or light they will lean in that direction.

Option two:

Simply point in the general direction of a body part you want to move and ask them "did you feel that".

If they reply no you reply "right there feel that" if they reply "yes I did" go with it, "right there in your knee (or whichever body part you choose)" it is getting stronger now bending. "That's right good job."

You may need to give the suggestion that that part gets more feeling as time passes and the more they think about it.

This is by far not fool proof but is a very good demonstration of "the POWER OF HYPNOSIS"

The Laughing Test

Often laughter is a good way to break the ice and this could not be more evident than with this test.

It works well in large groups and really does break the ice. The beauty of it is that people do not understand what is really going on and it baffles them.

It works on the same principle as a yawn going through a crowd. It is almost impossible not to laugh when others are doing it and once you get one or two people going you just pace and lead them.

This is one of my openers for high strung audiences and I love it.

The Effect

They hypnotist causes either one person or the whole audience to burst into spontaneous laughter which then feeds on itself.

How to

This works on the same principle as a yawn passing from one person to another. Ask the whole audience to

"Close your eyes and think of something funny and then begin to allow yourself to smile at the funny thing that has happened to you or someone you know. It is ok if a few people do not have the funny thing yet but they will and even if they do not someone near them is going to begin to laugh and they can find that funny because laughter is infectious and moves and grows from one person to another. More and more that's right growing expanding flowing more and more."

Continue to make these suggestions and indeed the laughter will spread from person to person and since the people's eyes are closed they do not know for sure how many people are actually laughing so it seems like the whole crowd. Also since people cannot see the others they assume others cannot see them and this lets them let go.

The Pen Lock

This is an old classic of both the therapy room and stage hypnosis. It has little to do with true hypnosis and a lot to do with muscle catalepsy.

The effect

The hypnotist locks a person's fingers on a pen so that they cannot let go.

How to

Subject holds a pen by index finger and thumb and you ask them to focus on the pen and refrain from blinking. Tell them to do exactly as instructed and start squeezing the pen tighter and tighter.

Tell them to think to themselves "I cannot drop it I cannot drop it" over and over without interruption. While they think this over and over tell them to try to drop the pen but the harder you try the tighter it gets

They find it will be impossible to drop the pen

The subject cannot let go of pen partially because of muscle catalepsy and partially because of suggestion.

Notes

This test also works if you get the person to focus on the words I am going to drop this Pen.

This test need not be performed with a pen in fact it can be performed with cards bottles or even jewellery if you so choose.

Impossible to get up from floor

While this test is good it also requires you to place your subject on the ground or floor. I am personally against both of those things.

Once again this test has nothing to do with hypnosis but it is the apparent use of mind control that causes it to look like hypnosis.

Effect

The hypnotist places person on floor and they are unable to get up from a lying position.

How to:

Ask the subject to either lie on the floor or place them there from a previous test. Place your index finger directly at the spot between their eyebrows and tell them to try to get up while applying slight pressure. This will cause them not to be able to get up.

Notes

There is a variant on this test from Ormond McGill's Encyclopaedia of stage hypnotism which uses a horse hair placed in the same place extending from the finger. This causes the illusion even to the subject that you are not touching them.

I PERSONALLY HAVE NOT USED THIS METHOD SO I AM UNABLE TO RECOMMEND IT BUT IT SOUNDS PROMISING.

Unable to bend leg

There is little in the world more alarming than losing one's sense of personal control. This test should be presented in a way that does not offend that worry. While not actually hypnosis it can look like hypnosis and is truly a wonderful test when done properly.

The Effect:

The hypnotist places subject in position and subject is unable to bend his leg.

How To:

Position subject in a standing position place your fingers on one side of the subjects head and tip it to one side. Hold their head in that position.

Place your other hand on their opposite hip keeping pressure on both the hip and head.

Now suggest that the side to which the head is tipped the leg is getting stiff and rigid. That he cannot bend the leg that he cannot even move it. He can try try try but will be unable to move it.

To end this test you remove the pressure and the subject is released.

Hand stuck to table or bottle or card or head or anything you want.

This is one of the many tests that street hypnotists use to prove the power of hypnosis. It has been used on television and in many trainings by some of the more current hypnotists and mentalists. It can be effective and is generally easy to do with the right subjects and the right knowledge.

Often the hypnotist will move from one stuck position to another for instance around a bottle to on a table to the persons head.

Effect:

A persons hand gets stuck to a using suggestion and cannot be moved.

How to:

Ask them which hand that they use and get them to put that hand flat on the table. Tell them to put their other hand off somewhere and just focus on the hand which is on the table.

Focus on just one spot and almost feel your hand melt into the table as you look at that point on your hand become aware of the table that you can see it, that you can feel it on the table. You can almost begin to feel the table pushing up on your hand and you can become fully absorbed as you feel the table pushing into your hand, I would like you to just imagine that glue is coming over your hand right now and as you imagine that you can focus now on the glue and how stuck your hand is becoming the fingers the palm all becoming stuck. Now.

In a few moments you can test your hand and make sure that it is stuck as now it becomes more and more stuck down tight to the table your hand and the table becoming one now.

You will only test it when you know it is stuck I will ask you to test it on the count of three one two three go ahead and test it harder ok now stop and allow it to release.

Name amnesia or making a person unable to say their name

This is a great test that I have used both on and off stage to great effect. Simply causing a person to forget their name draws a great response and can often be an amazing effect. Names are very personal things so make sure to give it back.

The Effect:

A person cannot say their name when asked.

How to:

Ask the person if they ever remember something they have forgotten a time when that thing was on the tip of their tongue but they just could not get it out. Ask them to think of their name and where there name would be if they could feel it on their body.

As they think about where that spot is get them to imagine their name as a cloud right there and get them to evaporate it into thin air. Making sure it is all gone disappearing from their mind and body floating away more and more.

Their name it is just gone from their mind unable to say it unable to remember the letters but it is right there on the tip of their tongue like a faded memory.

Go ahead try to say it, it is impossible.

And now the clouds reform into solid real letters and your name comes right back

Fingertip sticking

This test is often best done after a few of the other " sticking tests". Some of the audience may know how the magnetic fingers and even the magnetic hands works but this has no reason to other than real mind control.

The faster you do this test the better it usually works in my experience.

The Effect

People's fingers get stuck together and cannot be pulled apart.

How to:

Ask subjects to place their index fingers point to point and focus on the spot that they are touching each other look at that spot and nothing else.

Make sure they are pointing their fingertips at each other while they do this with their elbows at about 90 degrees otherwise this will not work.

Tell them that their fingers are now becoming glued together and in a few moments no matter how hard they try it will simply be impossible to get those fingers apart.

Those fingers are now becoming stuck tighter and tighter together and simply will not come apart. Go ahead try they simply will not come apart.

Release and they now come apart

Steel arm

This is a favourite of many hypnotists and is indeed a great way to convince the subject and the audience of "the Power" of hypnosis. Depending on your hypnotic character it may or may not suit you to use this test.

The Effect

The hypnotist makes passes power arm while giving suggestions and the subject cannot bend their arm.

How to

This test is similar in process to stiffening a person's leg.

Ask the subject to look into your eyes and extend their arm and make the muscles tense by making a fist.

Grab the subjects fist and pull it out slightly as you say "stiff, locking the joints, becoming stiffer and stiffer, and now it has become like a steel bar try as hard as you might you cannot bend it try, try harder now stop trying and release. "

Say all of this with confidence and believe in yourself. It may fail but the more you do it the more experience you get the better it will work as your confidence rises.

Note:

The reason the person looks into your eyes during this test is to create focus and awareness that you are in control.

Depending on your character and whether you play it as the power of hypnosis or as a normal person who can do some cool things then this test can have a drastic effect on your subjects.

Often hypnosis is about the subject buying into what you are doing and indeed allowing you to order them around.

Lemon test

This test demonstrates how the senses can be affected by suggestion alone. It is a great convincer for the whole audience and is an awesome way to break the ice.

The Effect

The hypnotist makes suggestions of the flavour of a lemon and the subject salivates and must swallow from the imagined lemon.

How to

Ask the subject to imagine eating a lemon the sour juices from the lemon on their lips and the bitter flavour sliding down their throat and the flavour on their tongue.

While doing this smack your lips together and salivate a little yourself for dramatic effect. This is also a Leading Motion for them to do the same.

Suggest this a few times in a row with different variants to the words and you will most likely have people salivating.

It is as simple as that in fact it worked on me just typing it out! This takes little practice and is easy to do enjoy.

Note:

This test can be used with almost any strong flavour or smell.

Hand to forehead

I have used this test in groups and as one on one test and it works very well in either situation. It is very startling to many individuals and is often seen as real mind control.

Effect

A persons hand comes towards their forehead as if by magnetic force.

How to

Place hand in air facing forehead a foot or so away slightly higher than head by about 3-5 inches.

Ask the volunteer to look at palm or the middle finger on their hand. Ask them to then imagine a magnet in their hand or finger and imagine steel plate in head.

Tell them the hand will come closer and closer the higher you count as the magnet gets stronger and stronger with each and every number and breath.

Note:

Sometimes I use a rope going through their head instead of a magnetic force. This test in itself can be used as an induction into hypnosis.

Cannot close mouth test

This is one test I have not used a lot as it does not suit my personality however it is included for completeness.

Effect:

The subject is told to open his or her mouth and then they cannot close it.

How to:

Ask the subject to open their mouth wide, wider and now it is becoming stuck open so stuck open that the subject simply cannot close it no matter how hard they try.

It is impossible to close your mouth no matter how hard you try.

Go ahead and try to close it. It will be impossible try, try. Now stop and relax the jaw and now you can close your mouth.

Impossible to open their mouth

This test is great as a gag with a person who is often to flamboyant for their own good. It can be a great joke but be sure not to offend by taking it to far.

The effect

After several other tests you perform this one and lock the persons mouth closed.

How to:

Ask the subject to focus directly on you and tell them to imagine a brush stroking their jaw. As they imagine this you say your lips are becoming stuck tight together stuck tighter and tighter. To the point where you cannot speak try to speak try, try harder. You are unable to speak because you cannot open your mouth.

The subject will try to speak but will be unable to do so.

And now relax your jaw and it will simply fall open as simple as that you can now speak, release.

Foot stuck to floor.

This test is fairly simple to preform and often knocks people for a bit of a loop. It can in fact be a very powerful demonstration of how hypnosis works.

The Effect

A person's foot gets stuck to the floor using just hypnotic suggestion.

How to:

Ask the person which hand is their dominant hand and get them to place that foot on the floor about 8 inches forward from the other foot.

Ask them to begin to imagine that their foot begins to stick to the floor. That they can imagine their leg beginning to lock tight and the tighter it locks the more hey realize just how stuck the foot becomes of course they could move it if they wanted to but they now know that it is becoming stuck down tight. The more they breathe the tighter it gets locked down more and more.

I want you to test your foot only when you are ready and you know it is locked down go ahead and test it on the count of three. That's right it is locked down tight. Stop trying and release that foot let it be free to move right now

Impossible to stand up

This test really has nothing to do with hypnosis and more to do with positioning of the subject. Like many pseudo hypnotic tests it is more about presenting apparent hypnosis than actual hypnosis.

The effect

A person cannot stand up from their chair

How to:

Ask a person to sit down in a chair and position them so that their legs are slightly out from the chair and their bum is forward slightly while they sit completely back in the chair. (As if they are lounging comfortable with bad posture.)

Place your index finger on the very center of their forehead just above the nose between the eyebrows and tell them you will sap their strength.

As you tell the subject to stand up press on the spot. This causes the subject to come off balance and they will not be able to stand no matter how hard they try.

To end this test simply take your finger away and say you are now released.

The Phantom rubber band

This is a one handed pre-test and works well with groups when finding those who you want to hypnotise for the show.

The Effect

A person's fingers on one hand come together at the hypnotists suggestions.

How to:

Ask the subjects to extend their hand or hands in front of them and extend the fingers all the way out in a "fan".

Ask them to strain the fingers as far as they will go and close their eyes.

Then ask them to start imagining a rubber band wrapped around those fingers getting tighter and tighter.

Go on for a few seconds and ask them to open their eyes.

Many in the audience will find that their fingers have come much closer together and in fact many people will have fingers that are touching or even unable to come apart.

Simply say relax and release the rubber band and the people's hands will be free to move.

Locked Hands

This test can be done one on one but in my experience works best in groups. There are 3 different variations.

1. In front with fists.

2. In front with hands pointed outwards.

3. Above head.

The Effect: Hands In Front with Fists

The hypnotist asks the spectator to place hands in praying position or straight in front position and through suggestion the person's hands are "stuck" together like a block of wood.

How to: In front with fists

Ask the spectator to intertwine their fingers and squeeze their hands together tell them to imagine hands as a solid block of wood or steel. You can either get them to close their eyes or keep them open.

Keep suggesting that the hands lock together tighter and tighter, as if a solid block of wood.

On the count of three those hands lock and no matter how hard you TRY you cannot get them apart.

One locking down tighter

Two locking down even tighter

Three tighter still go ahead try you cannot get them apart.

Locked Hands in front with palms pointed outwards.

The Effect: Hands In front with palms pointed outwards.

The hypnotist gets the spectator to place hands in front of them and intertwine fingers. The spectator then places hands and arms stretched outward and their hands are locked together.

How to: Hands In front with palms pointed outward.

Intertwine fingers and get person to place hands palms outwards and push out. This creates an automatic knuckle lock and just like the previous test you just mention that they are locking together.

Make suggestions that the person's hands are locked and they cannot come apart. Push your hands outwards locking tighter and tighter

It works by making it so the joints of the hands cannot pass past each other. It is a form of muscle catalepsy mixed with some very basic knowledge of human anatomy. This is a no fail test if performed properly.

The most important thing is that they continue to push out while trying to get "free" this locks the knuckles.

Locked Hands above head

The Effect: Hands In front with palms pointed outwards above head.

The hypnotist gets the spectator to place hands in front of them and intertwine fingers.

The spectator then places hands and arms stretched outward above their head and their hands are locked together.

How to: Hands In front with palms pointed outwards above head.

Intertwine fingers and get person to place hands palms outwards and above their head and push out.

This creates an automatic knuckle lock and just like the previous test you just mention that they are locking together.

Make suggestions that the person's hands are locked and they cannot come apart. Push your hands outwards locking tighter and tighter

It works by making it so the joints of the hands cannot pass past each other. It is a form of muscle catalepsy mixed with some very basic knowledge of human anatomy. This is a no fail test if performed properly.

The most important thing is that they continue to push out while trying to get

"free" this locks the knuckles.

Locked eyes/eyelid catalepsy

This is an easy and classic test and is used in many of today's fastest hypnotic inductions.

I like to do this with groups in the real format, there is a way to cheat and make it a simple body trick. I will teach you both ways.

The Effect: Locked Eyes/Eyelid Catalepsy

The spectator is told to close their eyes imagine that they cannot open their eyes and their eyes lids are locked down.

How to the real version:

Ask them to close their eyes. Imagine eyelids relax to the point they will not work. Or that glue is covering their eyes and hardening.

Tell them to try only when they are ready to open their eyes on the count of three.

They cannot open their eyes.

Tips & tricks

Don't say the word 3 in your count this creates confusion as to whether they should start testing or not.

Be fast do not test too long the shorter the better in my experience. Works awesome with groups or one on one

How to fake it version of the eye lock:

Ask them to close their eyes.

Turn their attention to the very top of their skull and try to look at it from inside their head.

Try to open their eyes it is simply impossible.

With the eyes pointed upwards they will simply not be able to open their eyes because their human physiology will not allow them to.

Both versions are safe and effective and have their place although one has absolutely no hypnosis involved.

Fall onto a chair

One of the greatest entertainers of a previous age the Amazing Kreskin did this on his old TV show the effect is old as the hills and relies on both hypnosis and human body science. It may even work without the hypnosis or suggestion.

The Effect

A person falls into chair as if an unseen force pushes them from the front.

How To

Position person so knees are touching the chair then you make motions towards them as if pushing "energy" towards them.

You can call it magnetic energy or a force or air. You tell them they will begin to feel it in their knees and they start tipping backwards. They then fall backwards onto the chair.

MAKE SURE THE CHAIR IS STABLE I SUGGEST HAVING SOMEONE BEHIND IT HOLDING IT AS TO PREVENT IT TIPPING.

In todays sue happy world it is better to be safe than sorry so be safe at all times.

Magnetic fingers

The Effect

A person's fingers come together when prompted by the hypnotist as if by a unknown force or HYPNOTISM.

How to

Place hands in front outstretched and interlock fingers then squeeze hands together with thumbs crossed at the back.

Point your index fingers out straight separate the fingers by one inch tell them that a magnetic force or rubber band is pulling the fingers together.

Fingers come together as if by magic.

This has absolutely nothing to do with hypnosis in fact it is an automatic body response and if the person is actually following the directions it cannot fail. If they do not follow directions it can fail but I have seen it work even then.

Fall back test

This test is used to be widely used all over the world and is now considered unusable due to danger by many hypnotists. The reason it is considered dangerous is because of improper training and general laziness on the part of many hypnotists. When performed properly it can be a hugely effective and dramatic is perfectly safe.

The main concern I have with this test is that you may have to put someone on the floor, and this is a health and safety concern for me personally. I would not want to be laid on a floor, I mean who knows what was on that floor in the first place.

Effect

This test makes people fall backwards into the hypnotist's arms or just wobble backwards until the hypnotist catches them.

There are two variations 1.Energy technique 2. Brushing head technique

How to

Stand a person up with feet together facing straight ahead. Ask them to watch your hand and imagine a force of energy pushing them coming from your hand. They will start to fall backwards. Have someone to catch them or catch them yourself.

You can accomplish this by "brushing" the side of their head as well and making the motions for them to fall backwards. It works on a person's sense of equilibrium and basically knocks them off balance.

Fall forward test

The same as fall backward test except you make the person fall forwards. There are two methods the 1.Energy technique and 2. Brush side of head technique

Effect

The hypnotist makes suggestions and hand passes and the subject falls forward.

How to

Stand a person up with feet together. Get them to look directly ahead with chin slightly up. Ask them to watch your hand and imagine a force of energy pulling them coming from your hand. They will start to fall forwards have someone to catch them or catch them yourself. If you are able bodied you may also take them down to the ground. I prefer not to do this as I do not like laying people on dirty floors. You can accomplish this by "brushing" the side of their head as well

Leaning test any direction

This test uses the same principle as fall test and is a good lead into the chair test. It can be based on energy or rope suggestions and can be used to lean a person forward or backwards.

Once again the first place I saw this performed was on The Amazing Kreskins old TV show and it was one of the best effects of the presentation.

The Effect

The subject leans forward or backwards by the will of the hypnotist teetering and wobbling for several seconds in different directions.

How to

Ask the person to stand straight with feet together place yourself in front of them and tell them to imagine a steel bar from your hand to their forehead slowly move your hand back and forth and they will follow your hand as it moves back and forth.

Fingertips will not touch

This is best used as a follow up to the fingertips sticking method.

Effect

A persons fingers will not touch tips.

How To:

Following the previous effect you say: Now take your fingertips and put them about 6 inches apart. Did you know your fingers can become nervous and shaky in fact they are becoming so nervous that they simply cannot touch one another right now.

More nervous now try to touch them to each other you cannot it is simply impossible..

Their fingers will simply not touch!

Missing finger/number

The ability to take someone's basic memory can be a lot of fun in this test we get a person to forget a number I find that the number six works best or me personally.

The Effect

A person counts their fingers and finds a number is missing

How To:

Ask the person if they ever remember something they have forgotten a time when that thing was on the tip of their tongue but they just could not get it out. Ask them to think the number six and bring that number to the front of their mind right to their forehead.

As they think about where that spot is get them to imagine the number as a cloud right there and get them to evaporate it into thin air. Making sure it is all gone disappearing from their mind and body floating away more and more as if it was pulled right out of them.

The number it is just gone from their mind now. You are unable to say it, unable to remember the number, but it is right there on the tip of their tongue like a faded memory pulled right out of your head..

Now let's count your fingers and see how many you have.

Count the fingers several times and watch the reaction to the effect.

And now the clouds reform into solid real letters and your name comes right back.

You can turn any pre-test into an induction it you know what to look for and the basics of doing this are simple. You get them to close their eyes and relax telling them to follow your suggestions. Some hypnotists will use a shock or confusion technique here but if they are already hypnotized (critical factor bypassed and following directions) to follow along with the pre-test to begin with then simply telling them to close their eyes and follow directions will often take them the rest of the way.

Once again the most important aspect of being a great hypnotist is having confidence in your hypnotic skills.

Induction at a ladies night (ladies nights are my favorite type of show)

Chapter 7: Stage inductions

In the past the stage hypnosis world was full of progressive relaxation inductions but thankfully that boring world has begun to change for better and worse in my opinion.

First why it is worse; it used to be that hypnosis was a process that everyone of a certain age knew had to take place and people expected to be hypnotized during that process. Previous hypnotic masters like Ormund Mcgill and Reveen set out and defined hypnosis for decades in North America at least. This was an accepted format but with all things faster and better comes along eventually. Some even say that the methods employed by old time hypnotists were out of date even when they were using them.

Second why it is better; the modern age of hypnosis in my opinion produces a better show even if it is somewhat shorter than our predecessors. Most hypnotists will produce a 60-90 minute show these days and it is entertainment from start to finish. This is good for the industry as no one gets bored but it also leads people of a certain age to think hypnosis does not exist because the process is not what they expect.

For those reasons we will look at various types of stage inductions both long progressive relaxations and medium rapids and into the "instant" inductions that are very popular today.

You should note that if you've used the pre-tests and it worked at all, that person is already in hypnosis by definition. They have followed your direction and all you really should have to do is continue giving acceptable suggestions. With this knowledge in hand you should not need to do a 20 minute progressive relaxation induction. Your induction should be much shorter and much more entertaining.

Let me state this clearly the only reason progressive relaxations are included in this in book is for completeness. If you choose to use them that's fine but it will make your show more boring. If your induction is any more than 10 minutes long you need to adjust it. In fact I would suggest if an induction is more than seven minutes long you need to adjust it. This is not to say longer inductions do not work however it is to say that from a modern audience's perspective progressive relaxations are just plain boring.

Progressive relaxation inductions:

A progressive relaxation induction is one that basically gets the person to relax their entire body from head to toe in sequence over the course of 8-45 minutes depending on the hypnotist.

One problem for me personally with progressive relaxations is that they are not reliable for me. Personally the faster an induction the better it works for me and my audiences.

It is important to note that the induction is a very big part of the show! In fact if you do not do one people will simply not believe you hypnotized anyone. No matter what you should include drama, comedy and theater into your inductions and in my opinion never go off mic during an induction as this creates a rift between you and the audience.

You will notice that all of the inductions are flowing and don't really have a break, that is because in many of the inductions you just keep talking and incorporating things into them. This creates confusion and helps bypass the critical factor.

Here is a progressive relaxation induction that could be used on stage if you so choose:

Hello everyone thank you for coming up, are you all ready to be hypnotized? Awesome, tonight we are going to put you in a trance and relax you so please just take a deep breath. Awesome, now close your eyes and listen to the sound of my voice.

First focus your attention and imagine a bright white light at the very top of your head and allow it to make your mind and body begin to relax. First focus on the muscles in the top of your head and let them relax.

Following each and every suggestion I give from this point forward going deep into relaxation. Now allowing your face to relax and all of those tiny muscles around your eyes to go loose limp and relaxed.

Letting that relaxation drop down all the way through your neck and into your shoulders. Focusing on those shoulders and letting them relax as the light splits and goes through your upper arms and into your fore arms and hands relaxing them as it comes back up to your shoulders and you take a deep breath and go deeper.

Every breath from this point forward just takes you deeper and deeper relaxed allowing your chest muscles to relax now. Allowing that light to just go through you down through your upper back and then into your lower back relaxing all those tiny tense little muscles.

Floating down now down into your stomach letting all of your abdominal muscles relax completely and totally every little muscle nerve and fiber goes down deeper and deeper relaxed. Now focus your attention on your hips and just let them relax as light continues down through your legs and your calves and knees through your ankles relaxing your feet all the way to the very tips of your toes.

Today is gone tomorrow as 1000 miles away and you can imagine a stairway in your mind the just continues going down and down and down this is the stairway of relaxation and now as you take a very deep breath you realize that with each and every breath you take it's just another step down the stairway allowing you to relax letting every suggestion go into your mind and body.

Following my suggestions quicker and easier than you ever thought possible allowing your mind to just drift and float as if it's on a cloud take a deep breath in and go down another step deeper relaxed the deeper you go the better you feel the better you feel the deeper you will go and as you begin the follow each and every single suggestion I give quicker and easier than the last you realize just how good it feels to relax allowing your muscles to go loose limp and relaxed again and a deep breath in as you imagine taking another step down that awesome stairway of relaxation.

The lights is still there and it can float up and down your body relaxing more and more feeling calm. Remaining seated in your chair at all times not falling out no matter how relaxed you get. now that you can just drift and float and float and drift within your heart's content allowing yourself to just let go focusing your attention right now on your left pinky finger it is something weird to focus your attention on but you might notice you have a little bit of tension there and you can just stretch it out and get rid of that tension.

You might find that you need to swallow and if that's the case go ahead or you might find that your nose is a little bit itchy and if that's the case you can go ahead and scratch while continuing to go deeper and deeper relaxed..

Following each and every suggestion as you float within your own mind drifting and floating down. Going deeper and deeper relaxed from this moment forward everything I say to you instantly becomes your reality and you will follow each and every single suggestion that I give quicker and faster than you ever thought possible sinking deeper into hypnosis now.

Allow yourself to take in a steep breath in and just drop down now deeper more relaxed and more suggestive to everything I say. During the show you will be very active acting on every suggestion using your body your mind and your voice to comply with every suggestion I give knowing of course that you won't do anything against your moral compass drifting down further now.

In a few moments I will say the words sleep now and that's your cue to go a million times deeper relaxed. Anytime I say the words sleep now from this point forward if your eyes were open your head would simply fall forward and just your eyes close and go million times more deeper relaxed.

Of course if you are standing when I said those words sleep now you would not fall down you would be completely and totally stable except that your head would fall forward on your chest your eyes closing and you will completely loose limp and relaxed except you would remain standing.

In a few moments I will get you to open your eyes look directly at me and say the words sleep now when I do your eyes will close your head will fall forward on your chest and you will go a million times more deeper relaxed one two three eyes open look directly at me and a deep breath in - sleep now that's right deeper relaxed.

Let's do this a few more times 123 eyes open look right at me sleep now deeper relaxed.

Let's do it again 123 eyes open sleep now deeper relaxed. 123 sleep now deeper relaxed. 1 ---- 2------ 3 sleep now deeper relaxed.

Following each and every suggestion I give from this point forward quicker and easier and less let's move on ladies and gentlemen to the very first skit of the night. In a moment you will begin to imagine that you are …. And on with the show.

And that's a progressive relaxation induction, my goodness is that boring. On top of that the whole induction itself could be made a lot simpler by getting rid of the filler and turning it into a rapid induction:

Everyone look right at me. Awesome now close your eyes. Focus your attention on the sound of my voice. Allow yourself to relax your eyelids as much as possible and let that quality of relaxation go through your entire body.

That is the entire relaxation process done in about 15 seconds. Then to finish the induction:

From this moment forward everything I say to you instantly becomes your reality and you will follow each and every single suggestion that I give quicker and faster than you ever thought possible sinking deeper into hypnosis now.

During the show you will be very active acting on every suggestion using your body your mind and your voice to comply with every suggestion I give.

In a few moments I get you to open your eyes you will look directly at me and I will say the word sleep now when I do your eyes will close your head will fall forward on your chest and go million times more deeper relaxed.

1 2 3 eyes open look directly at me and a deep breath in sleep now that's right deeper relaxed. Let's do this a few more times 123 eyes open look right at me sleep now deeper relaxed. Let's do it again 123 eyes open sleep now deeper relaxed. 123 sleep now deeper relaxed. 1 ---- 2------ 3 sleep now deeper relaxed.

Following each and every suggestion I give from this point forward quicker and easier and less let's move on ladies and gentlemen to the very first skit of the night. In a moment you will begin to imagine that you are .... And on with the show.

I have done this short of an induction many times but have run into one problem when it is only 30 seconds long. People don't believe it then! So my induction is a classic modified Elman with a lot of entertainment thrown in so it is not boring.

My version of the modified Elman induction for stage

Focus your attention right now on me look right at me. Close your eyes relax. Open your eyes look at me. Close your eyes relax. Open your eyes look at me. Close your eyes relax.

Now you may find this silly and that's right just keep those eyes closed and focus your attention right now on the sound of my voice no noise around the room will bother you in any way shape or form in fact it just allows you to relax more.

In a few moments you will go into hypnosis and when you do you will feel fantastic for the rest of the night. I would like you to focus your attention on your left foot and notice any sensations whatsoever in that left foot. Know that they are completely and totally natural for you.

I would like you to think of something funny in your mind maybe something that happened to you today maybe this very situation you're in right now and as you do you can allow yourself to smile at whatever that funny thing is.

If a smile comes your face you may notice a little bit of laughter and if you want you can let that laughter out because if you do you going to find that your laughter is infectious and it will affect everyone else and in when somebody else laughs near you I'm not sure when it will happen but it will you'll find that you laugh at their laughter as you allow it to get funnier and funnier within your own mind following each and every suggestion I give from this point forward quicker and easier than the last.

Now focus your attention on your eyes and allow them relax completely and totally little muscle nerve and fibre and let that quality relaxation for all the way down to the very tips of your toes throughout your entire body.

As you do I'm going to come some of you lift up your hand and drop it back onto your lap when I drop it that's just your cue to relax completely and totally every little muscle nerve and fibre.

If I don't come to that's fine it just means that I didn't come to you. That's right let that hand be loose limp and relaxed like a wet dishcloth. Just let it plop right back on down on your knee. Perfect deeper relaxed.

Now I would like you to focus your attention the number 100 as you focus your attention the number 100 imagine it as a cloud in your mind now its your job to allow yourself to have mental relaxation and push that cloud away from you each breath you take makes you go deeper. Deep breath now and just let that cloud be pushed away from you evaporate it.

I will continue to count down and as I do I want you push those clouds away from you to and as you push them away your mind will just relax following each and every suggestion I give from this point forward quicker and easier than the last. 99 deeper relaxed today is gone tomorrow's 1000 miles away 98 deeper relax all stress floating away from you right now 96 deeper relaxed pushing those clouds of your mind further and further away 92 pushing those clouds away from you completely.

In a few moments I'm going to say the word sleep now when I do your head will fall forward your eyes will remain closed you will go a million times more deeper relaxed 123 sleep now.

In a few moments I will get you to open your eyes I will say the word sleep now when I say the words sleep now your head will fall forward on your chest your eyes will close and you will go million times more deeper relaxed 123 eyes open sleep now.

Deeper relaxed. 123 eyes open sleep now deeper relaxed. One… Two… Three… Eyes open sleep now. In a few moments were going to continue with the show when I count from 1 to 3 you will believe _____

And we would move on with the show. This induction incorporates several things first off it's believable to the audiences that I work with.

It takes just long enough between two minutes and six minutes not to be boring. It's not dangerous. It's highly effective provided you believe in yourself. It incorporates several hypnotic phenomenon and some hypnotic language. Above all that it's entertaining to watch.

This induction has action from the very start that act as tests for you and convincers for the subjects. The laughter test from the pre-tests is actually built right into my modified Elman.

This is not only entertaining it means they have action taking place right away during the actual induction within the first 30 seconds. Because of this people often do not realize an induction has actually happened.

Sometimes the laughter skit is actually a longer period than the actual induction itself. This induction works for me and it is my go to induction for most shows.

But what about something flashier! You want more Pizzaz! You want instant inductions! You can do instant inductions with almost all of the pre-tests that were listed in the chapter on pre-tests.

Instant inductions once you know how to do them are extremely simple but first you must understand some basic information:

IF A SUBJECT TAKES ONE SUGGESTION, GENERALLY THEY WILL TAKE THEM ALL PROVIDED THEY ARE IN CONTEXT.

This means that if you have done a good pre-talk and are now doing magnetic fingers and they are watching their fingers move closer together and you get them to just close their eyes and say sleep now. Chances are they will continue to follow your suggestions. Wild right! BUT …. You have to continue to give deepening suggestions that they can follow. So it would go like this:

Awesome are you ready to experience hypnosis nod your head yes. Good now put your hands together like this and cross your thumbs at the back.

Now squeeze your hands together tightly and point your index fingers out and squeeze them together.

Do not do this yet but in a moment on the count of three I will get you to pull your index fingers apart not all of your fingers just the index ones about one inch. When I do you will almost feel a magnetic pull on your fingers an irresistible force compelling them back together. 1 2 3 pull those index fingers apart and imagine that force pulling them back together.

Squeeze those palms together and watch those fingers start to move. Imagine it happening… Want it to happen and it will… awesome and when they come together drop your hands just close your eyes and relax deeper following every suggestion I give from this point forward.

Notice that this should take about 30 seconds maximum to accomplish 1 on 1 and less than a minute if doing it as a group stage induction and at no time was the word sleep even necessary.

In fact the word sleep is really just used as an anchor/cue in most hypnosis shows to make people go back to the "hypnosis position" that society expects.

This type of induction is really valuable as a "real world induction" when you want to do hypnosis off stage for entertainment purposes.

There are many other types of inductions and you can use them separately or together with other inductions to make them more effective.

If you are using the instant style inductions on stage and you are good at them you can use them as your primary induction as you choose. How do you get good: PRACTICE ON REAL PEOPLE. Grab your courage and just do it.

Other ways to do instants in a more dramatic fashion is to do shock inductions. This is an induction where you get a subject to focus on something and then give them a slight shock. These inductions include the arm pull or drop and can look very dangerous. The thing to remember is that the shock does not have to be a big one. If you are doing and arm pull the pull only needs to be about a one inch one and you can do it very gently and it still looks good and shocks the person.

The theory of doing shock inductions is that when you give the shock or jostle the subject they have a brief moment where the critical factor bypassed. About 1/10 of a second is all you have, so if you say sleep exactly when you jostle them and give them a deepener afterwards theoretically they will go into hypnosis. This does take practice and does not work every time which is part of the reason why I choose not to use them in my show. The second part of the reason why I don't use in my show is because they can look dangerous and for my specific clientele that is a big no-no.

If you're working in a comedy club or bar they may be appropriate. For corporate's I would never do them, for schools I would never do them, for fairs I would never do them and anywhere else that needs to look super safe I would never do them.

In the case study section you will be given information to look up several stage hypnotists' full shows. The shows are freely available on the Internet for you to view. Many of these hypnotist actually are trainers and their only income comes from the show's they do. I would highly suggest you look at each of them up and do the exercises for reviewing your show as if you were reviewing their show for improvement. By doing this you can see what works for them and create your own show for yourself. You then have a good understanding of what a live hypnosis show looks like and the ability to critique your own show. This is not to steal their stuff but model it and create your own show.

Here is a basic shock induction:

DO A GOOD PRETALK and several pre-tests on the subject. If you are in a group setting do several group pre-tests with the whole group before doing this. This establishes proof in your subjects mind and they are more likely to be suggestible to the induction.

(Stand in front of them) Look right here (point just under your eye)

(Place your hands on their shoulders) Focus now as you look here

(Place hand on the back of their head cradling it) Are you ready to go into hypnosis… (wait for them to nod their head) good (tap back of head with your middle finger) SLEEP NOW

Other shock inductions are also available and you will see several types used if you watch the hypnotists in the homework section.

Now that you have an understanding of how different inductions work let's move onto show structure!

Chapter 8: Skits and show structure

This could be the most important chapter in the book for those who have been performing for a while because it will give you distinct insights on how you can improve your show. If you have never performed, at the end of this chapter is some very important homework for you to do that will give you a great kick start to developing your own show.

A show is generally divided into three important parts:

1. The Pre-talk and induction
2. The Skits
3. The Closing

We have already looked at the pre-talk and induction. This chapter is all about the skits and putting them together. There are two main ways to look at the skits and direction of your show. They each have their benefits. Let's look at them.

1. The no direction, go as you flow show.
2. The story show.

The no direction show

The no direction show is basically a bunch of skits thrown together and you can do whatever comes to your mind. It is free flowing and can be a huge hit. This adds to the spontaneity of the show.

The story form show

This is my preferred show style, it weaves a story through the show and gives a more uniform appearance with theatrical structure. I prefer this style as my show is motivational in nature and I can weave motivation in to a show much easier with a story than I can by having random unattached skits. It also allows me to have a definitive ending that is a climax to the show and everyone knows it is the end.

There are thousands of skits to choose from! If you do an internet search you will find that there are a lot of skits out there and most hypnotists are using a lot of the same ones. If you look deeper you will find that they perform them the same way. This is sad as it does not allow for you to have your own show just a cheap copy of a cheap copy. In my opinion you should create your own show and yes you can use those old tried and true skits but for goodness sake make them your own. How do you do that? Here is what I do to create as much entertainment value from a skit as possible.

SKIT EXPANSION EXERCISE:

First give yourself permission to write as much craziness as possible. Say I _____ give myself permission to be creative and downright crazy during this creative process.

Next think of a basic skit:

_____

Next think of as many things as you can that could happen on a beach:

- Who is there
- What is happening
- What cloithes are the people wearning
- The Smells
- The Tastes
- The Animals
- Temperature
- Sights

- Actions they can do
- Products they could use
- Anything else

Then list as many specific actions people could take as possible no matter how crazy it may seem.

1.

2.

3.

4.

5.

6.

7.

8.

9.

10.

This gives you a whack of possibilities for every skit you have and you can use it to outline your skit so it is unique to you. Now it is time for you to outline your basic show. Pick at least 6 general skits for your show.

1.
2.
3.
4.
5.

6.

If you cannot think of six possible skits, go online and look up "hypnosis show skits" this should bring up a large list of skits that you can pick and choose from.

Once you have your skits then go through them with the skit expansion exercise and expand them with it as much as possible. Then put them into a format from easiest to hardest and you have your show laid out in front of you.

YOUR skit expansions:

Skit 1 _____

- Who is there

  _____
  _____
  _____

- What is happening

  _____
  _____
  _____

- What clothes are the people wearing

  _____
  _____
  _____

- The Smells

  _____
  _____
  _____

- The Tastes

  _____

_____

- The Animals

_____

_____

- Temperature

_____

_____

- Sights

_____

_____

- Actions they can do

_____

_____

- Products they could use

_____

_____

- Any thing else

_____

_____

_____

Skit 2 _____

- Who is there

_____

- What is happening

  _____

  _____

  _____

- What clothes are the people wearing

  _____

  _____

  _____

- The Smells

  _____

  _____

  _____

- The Tastes

  _____

  _____

  _____

- The Animals

  _____

  _____

  _____

- Temperature

  _____

  _____

  _____

- Sights

  _____

  _____

  _____

- Actions they can do

  _____

  _____

  _____

- Products they could use

  _____

  _____

  _____

- Any thing else

  _____

  _____

  _____

Skit 3 _____

- Who is there

  _____

  _____

  _____

- What is happening

  _____

  _____

  _____

- What clothes are the people wearing

  _____

  _____

  _____

- The Smells

  _____

  _____

  _____

- The Tastes

  _____

_____

- The Animals

_____
_____
_____

- Temperature

_____
_____
_____

- Sights

_____
_____
_____

- Actions they can do

_____
_____
_____

- Products they could use

_____
_____
_____

- Any thing else

_____
_____
_____

Skit 4 _____

- Who is there

_____

- What is happening

  _____

- What clothes are the people wearing

  _____

- The Smells

  _____

- The Tastes

  _____

- The Animals

  _____

- Temperature

  _____

- Sights

  _____

- Actions they can do

  _____

  _____

  _____

- Products they could use

  _____

  _____

  _____

- Any thing else

  _____

  _____

  _____

Skit 5 _____

- Who is there

  _____

  _____

  _____

- What is happening

  _____

  _____

  _____

- What clothes are the people wearing

  _____

  _____

  _____

- The Smells

  _____

  _____

  _____

- The Tastes

  _____

_____

- The Animals

_____
_____
_____

- Temperature

_____
_____
_____

- Sights

_____
_____
_____

- Actions they can do

_____
_____
_____

- Products they could use

_____
_____
_____

- Any thing else

_____
_____
_____

Skit 6 _____

- Who is there

_____

_____

- What is happening

_____

_____

- What clothes are the people wearing

_____

_____

- The Smells

_____

_____

- The Tastes

_____

_____

- The Animals

_____

_____

- Temperature

_____

_____

- Sights

_____

_____

- Actions they can do

  _____

  _____

  _____

- Products they could use

  _____

  _____

  _____

- Any thing else

  _____

  _____

  _____

Now if you want you could just use these skits as is without a story structure. If you choose to go the story style show route you would simply think of a reason these things are happening in a logical order from each other. For instance:

Bed skit - They are sitting in bed and must get up so they do silly getting up things-> Driving skit - this leads them to taking a drive ->Movie skit - this leads them to the movies-> Celerity skit - this leads them to becoming a celebrity-> this leads to dancing with the stars.

Of course everything is expanded with the skit expansion exercise but has a logical reason for happening. If you want to get weird like me in many of my shows I use a unicorn exploding for a reason for stuff happening. The unicorn explodes and gives them magical or super powers like playing the banjo, x-ray vision, and an itch they cannot scratch. It makes the show into a continuity instead of just a bunch of skits thrown together.

Create your own show and give it reasons for happening if you would like to create a story style of show. It is what I have done and some will tell you it is too scripted out but it works for me.

Many say a scripted show is a bad thing and I highly disagree, and agree at the same time. My show does have a flow and I like to keep it the same, however I am able to adjust to the groups needs. If I see a skit not working I change to a different one and move on. There have been times when I do my opening skit get little response and move on to the next skit and get a great response.

Being your own director

I record every single show I do these days. There are a couple of reasons the first one is for insurance purposes. The second is so I can critique my show.

Every month me and my wife randomly choose 3 shows from the previous month and dissect them to find the weak spots. We run through them and are really mean about it. She makes me cry…

Why be mean to yourself you ask? Well you need to be your own director. If you are doing something that you don't like it you can bet others HATE it. But they will not tell you about it at all.

Right after the show you will get all of the "that was the funniest thing I have ever seen comments" but a week later no one will be there to give you real feedback.

So for the benefit of my show I break it down and really have improved my show over time.

So it is now time for you to improve your show over time. I use this form below to improve my performances and you can use it too.

Show Date_____ Show Time _____

Venue _____

What was the reaction to your walk out and introduction? Where can it improve?

_____

_____

What was the reaction to your Pretalk? Where can it improve?

_____

_____

What was the reaction to your Routines?

_____

_____

_____

_____

_____

_____

Post hypnotics

_____

_____

Were there new routines

_____

_____

_____

List the biggest reactions during the show and review their wording

_____
_____
_____

List the least reaction and review their wording

_____
_____
_____

What areas do you need to work on to improve the show next time.

_____
_____
_____

List three things you will improve and practice before your next performance

1. _____
2. _____
3. _____

This form will give you an accurate and easy way to improve your show and I would suggest when you start out doing it every show and after about 50 shows do it every 5 or so shows from then on. This will give you a huge crash course and destroy your learning curve to getting a kick ass stage hypnosis show put together.

Training the audience!

The truth about audiences is that they need to be trained. We have been watching TV since the 60's and it has degraded our ability to be a good live audience. Most people will not clap at their TV, they will not laugh out loud at their TV, most will sit like bumps on logs and not react at all with their TV which let's face it that is only right because a TV is a box in your home that sound and lights shoot out of.

A live show on the other hand is a living breathing entity and relies on your audience as much as the volunteers to make the show. Without good audience reaction your show can fall flat and there are several ways to get it.

Want proof go watch a live recorded event on television and watch how they get the audience involved. (once again I recommend a wrestling program.) This is true for almost all forms of entertainment. The original reason a laugh track was put on TV was so people knew what was funny and what was not. You don't get that luxury so train your audience.

1. The clapping gag

With this you get a volunteer from the audience to come up and put their hands out in front of them. Then ask the whole audience to do the same thing. Then you say "well everyone now that I have you in this position if you enjoy the show today what do you think you are going to do." Someone will clap. You praise them and move on. It is a not so subtle reminder that they are part of the show too.

2. Audience pump ups

You come out to music that is energized and you get people to start clapping their hands and getting the energy up in the room.

3. Telling them straight out to give some applause

Yes just plain and simple asking for applause. The simple fact is many younger groups have no idea when to applaud and the older ones fear that they could break the hypnotic spell by applauding. Use your hypnotic powers and just ask for it.

4. Make them laugh

Yes just making someone laugh gives others permission to laugh too. So use this against them and make just one person laugh and you will do just fine.

5. Call someone out

Do you see that guy with the crossed arms, ask him if he hates you and explain that basic body language says he is mad at something. Did he pee his pants, is he constipated, did his puppy get run over. Be nice about it especially if you have no clue who he is. You do not want to embarrass the CEO of a company right! This lets the others in the audience know that they are a part of it and if they don't want to be called out

Nurturing entertainment value

There are two sins in comedy hypnosis

1. Going on with a gag or skit way too long.

2. Not going long enough and it is the hardest thing in the world to gauge at the time.

I would suggest to you that once you have performed a couple of shows your timing will improve and you will get better but for now I suggest you not have any skits that last over 8 minutes by themselves and even that is a long skit. Especially in a 1 hour show. TV has taught us over the years to work at and understand a faster pace than previous generations. It is up to you to make your show as entertaining as possible.

Sometimes I find myself having fun with a skit but notice the audience is just sitting there not doing anything. When this happens it is either time to move on or create an audience interaction moment.

Controlling the moment

You are the director on stage and because of that you can direct attention. If you see something funny happening you should point it out. If you see something dangerous give a distracting suggestion and go deal with it. There can be no excuses, in the end ,that stage is yours.

Own the whole room

Look around you where ever you are and get present, focus your attention and imagine your presence expanding to fill the room. Now do this every day because it is your job to give the guy 40 rows back the same experience as the guy in the front row.

They should feel part of the show and be a part of the show as much as anyone. Understand you need to be the alpha in that room and have control.

There is no room for compromise be CEASAR and control the world (well at least the room) this will get rid of about 99 percent of hecklers too.

Getting rid of the weak

118

Do you have someone not listening to you? Get rid of them and have no fears about it. When I first started I wanted a full stage of volunteers to stay up there because it looks better. Now I don't care, my only job is to entertain and have fun. Get rid of the fakers and the idiots you do not need them anyway.

How to have multiple climaxes KINKY!

Multiple climaxes are essential to any hypnotic performance and you should try to achieve them. The easiest way is to plan out your skits and understand what is going to happen in advance. Think of it this way, when you write a play (any play: think Broadway) it is generally divided into three acts. These acts constitute the hero's journey and each act has a climax with the final climax of course coming at the end. That is how I like to format my show so it has a proper flow and finality to the whole thing.

This gives the audience a better experience in my opinion and I do this for all of my performances. Does it ever go off on a tangent? Of course! But that is why you are a hypnotist and entertainer so you can create the show you want.

All of these multiple climaxes are achieved through a properly scripted show and understanding what goes into each portion to make it great!

Scripting a proper show

We have already went through your pre-talk, but what about the skits, how will you give suggestions? What voice tones will you use? What will your body movement be? These things are all important and should be considered. I would suggest writing out a full show and practicing it 10-100 times before you even step foot on stage. Will it get boring? Yes, but it will also allow you the much needed time to actually see where your suggestions are not as strong.

The more you immerse yourself in practice the better. When I first started, before my first show, I would practice my full show – pre-talk, induction, skits, closing all of it 3 times per day for a full two weeks. Why only two weeks? Well because I followed my mentors advice and booked a show before I was ready and that is the advice I am going to give you too.

BOOK A SHOW RIGHT NOW BEFORE YOU ARE READY!

The exercise you did before will have you doing most of this already so you are ahead of the game. Now it is your time and mission to put in the real work to accomplish your goals and make the show an absolute killer performance.

GO BOOK A FREAKING SHOW

Yes right now you should be thinking about booking your show. If you are not ready I don't care fail-forward and just do it. If you never start you will never start. By this point you already have the hypnotic tools at your disposal, now all you need to do is book the show and put them to use. So do it! Go to the section on booking your first show and book 1-10 shows. Preferably 10 so you have motivation.

Now know that you cannot cancel them PERIOD. Because that is not you, you are an entertainer, you are the hypnotist, you are great and it would be ethically wrong to book a show and not show up.

I see entertainers all the time not showing up to booked events. This is the stupidest thing on earth. SHOW UP TO YOUR F-ING EVENT. It is just good business and if you don't whoever is there will never hire you again and you personally lose credibility for any future events.

It also makes the whole industry look bad so please show up.

Since 2007 I have missed 1 event because of a scheduling screw up with an agency. Guess what they have never hired me again. I broke their trust and I deserve not to be hired. (Even if the fault was on their end and they just don't know it.)

In total it has cost me 1000's of dollars they used to book me for about $10000 worth of shows per year. I don't know many people who would not like an extra $10000 with very little work going into it.

Choosing quality material for your audience

Before you ever perform you need to ask yourself who your general audience is going to be and what is suitable for them. This will give you a better understanding of what is actually appropriate for them and for you personally.

One thing to consider is also what is appropriate for the venue in which you are performing. There is a market for every type of show and sometimes performing in one market will prevent you from performing in another so be careful with your material.

The rules I follow for my performances is that I do a clean show and nothing else. What this means is no violence, no swearing, no nudity. This allows me to work the clean markets like schools, fairs, associations, and corporations where being clean is at the forefront of their needs. For other groups being clean is not necessary but I would still ask and never go too far. Comedy clubs, bars, casinos, and others may actually want a dirtier show. It really depends on your preferences and your audiences preferences. If you want to get booked again and again give them what they want.

Your appearance

DAMN YOU ARE UGLY, Just kidding! You are just fine the way you are but it is important to enhance your appearance as much as you can for a hypnosis show. For me that is simply wearing a suit and tie and (don't tell anyone) make-up.

Yes I wear cover up. The general rule of thumb for me is to dress 2 levels above the general audience. This puts you among the best dressed in the room category but not too fancy that people will feel offended.

Why 2 levels above the general audience? Because it gives you an air of authority and establishes you as the stand out immediately. One of the largest considerations of how well you will be able to hypnotize others is how they view you. Are you an authority? Are you an expert? Are you the hypnotist? Dress the part.

NO I do not mean all black with a pointy goatee and a watch, but dress like you are a hypnotist and know what the hell you are doing. The first step to being a good hypnotist is giving them something they can relate to a hypnotist and it is really easy from there.

Your voice

You voice is important and you need to know how to use it properly, there are many ways to use your voice to create emotion, atmosphere and drama. Use it to do so, hypnosis is not something that should be monotone at all. In fact you should use your voice in a way that may get through their critical factor and place them into hypnosis. It is really just another tool you can use to create a better show.

EXERCISE:

Use your voice and give suggestions to make them more dramatic and emotional.

Write out 5 "happy suggestions" and give them in a monotone voice

1.

2.

3.

4.

5.

Now give them with laughter and happiness in your voice! Notice the difference in how you feel and how the words feel to you. Even fake happiness creates real happiness.

Write out 5 "sad suggestions" and say them with a monotone voice:

1.

2.

3.

4.

5.

Now say them as if you are sad ham it up as much as you can and see how it makes you feel.

Write 5 exciting suggestions and say them monotone:

1.

2.

3.

4.

5.

Now say them with excitement in your voice.

Write 5 dramatic suggestions

1.

2.

3.

4.

5.

Now say them with drama in your voice.

I am not writing this all to waste trees I am writing all of it to make you a better performer. If you are not excited, if you are not dramatic, if you are not happy or sad along with the show then why the hell am I or your audience watching you.

When you add inflection to your suggestions it also gives your volunteers a bit more direction where to go with it as far as their skills on stage. This can help a lot with performers finding themselves with a "flat" show. There are a lot of hypnotists out there that are really not performing he best shows because they just have never taken the time to think these things through.

Give your performance "LIFE". You are not a computer that just spits out words in a monotone are you? So use your humanity and be a performer, be an entertainer and for god's sake entertain with your natural talents and abilities!

Comedy moments and Improv

This is really what most stage hypnosis is all about comedy and getting people to do funny things but you also need to be willing to do anything to get that laugh. I do recommend to every entertainer to take an improv class and acting lessons if possible it will make you a better performer in general. For right now I have some exercises you can do with your friends that are easy and fun. Using these excercises you have a basis for improv and can then react more fluidly to your stage hypnosis situations.

Exercise:

Grab a buddy or six and start making a story one person at a time. The first person starts with once upon a time and the next follows with one sentence in the story and so on and so on. This hones your skills to adapt and create something amazing on the fly. Keep going for about 10 minutes and you will find that the origin has nothing to do with the ending and if nothing else it was fun doing the exercise.

Know your audience

That's right know your audience! Who makes up your general audience? What do they know and think about hypnosis?

What will they find funny?

What do you need to give them for a great performance?

What level of maturity do they have?

Are they uptight?

Do you need to break the ice or can you just go for whatever you want to do?

Do you have to keep it a certain rating (G, PG, PG14, etc.)

If you can answer these questions before you walk on stage you will be much further ahead of the game.

So stop for a minute and do the following exercise:

Ask yourself and write down the answers to the previous questions in regards to:

For a corporate audience

For a school audience

For a comedy club

For a service club

For a collage

For a ladies night

For a mens night

Each audience is different and it is a good idea to make some general assumptions and be prepared for that audience type. This is especially true if you are just starting out.

Make up

Should you wear make up? That depends do you look good? Imagine this: I walk out on stage with my bald head and the light hits it like a disco ball in 1976. BAM half of my audience goes blind and the other half into convulsions.

OK it has never happened and never will but it gets my point across. The lights show EVERY THING, every blemish, every pimple, every scar, and the easiest way to say it is YOU UGLY. Just kidding but we can always make ourselves look better with a little bit of makeup!

Are you oily? Do you have blotches? I do have blotches and I do wear makeup as cover up on some shows. We are in show business and no one wants to watch a blotchy person hypnotizing people so try to be as nice looking as possible.

A good cover up is all most people need to look ok in front of an audience and even out their skin tones. It does not make you less of a man to wear a little make up sometimes and you will find by looking better people trust you more as well.

One note is men are really not used to wearing makeup and it can get quite hot on stage. Therefore carry something to wipe yourself with as a large spot of makeup on your suit is very noticeable.

Using music in your show to set the mood before the show

Music can enhance or hinder a hypnosis show depending on what you are trying to accomplish in regards to entertainment value. My music playlist lasts about 1 hour and is suitable for everyone. The music I choose has a specific purpose and that is to relax and put people in the mood to have fun. When you choose your preshow music make sure it fits your persona and gets you in the mood to perform as well.

One thing you may want to avoid is scary creepy music as it can often ruin a show. People these days really are not finding hypnosis as mysterious as it once was and don't want to feel unhinged just before a show. There is a place for this if you are doing other kinds of shows like a hypnotic séance or spook show for example and in that context creepy music should be fine. Just be careful if you do choose to play a funeral march beforehand and know that people will be in a state that you probably will not be able to do anything with if it is in the wrong context.

It is important to stay congruent with the feeling of your show and by far the most common type of hypnosis show is the comedy hypnosis type.

Using music in your actual show

Music can enhance and add to the experience of the show and in my opinion is essential if you want to have a great show. There are many hypnotists that do not use music and that is fine but for mine I have to have it. I have done it both ways and highly prefer to have music.

127

Music is a few things first it can cover slow moments for when you're calling volunteers, it can build tension, enhance comedy, and single climaxes. Kinky! Music can also play a specific role in the hypnotic process itself by overwhelming other sounds.

With specific music you can create an atmosphere that's funny, inspirational, dramatic, soothing, romantic, or any other emotion you want to convey. When choosing your music it's important to start with the end in mind and only then search for the music that fits what you want to do.

Sometimes a performer can make a mistake with their music by not using it in the right way. An example is really dramatic music for when you call volunteers up on stage. This creates a tense atmosphere and is not conducive to the performance of hypnosis. You should be thinking your music through from start to finish for the entire show if you're going to use it because while good music can enhance the performance bad music can turn it into a big steaming pile of dog turd.

Having a real entertainment experience that includes lots of different entertainment touch points is the real key to having a great hypnotic show and in this portion of the book we are going to look at different types of entertainment touch points you can have during your hypnosis show.

Action it's all that matters

Lights camera action is the old Hollywood saying and it is even more important to have action on stage when performing a show then it is in the film. You see action can be a great way to entertain your audience, whether it's your actions, your body language, your manner, or the actions you have your volunteers going through it all adds to the entertainment value.

When you're planning your show you should think about the action, the movement, and the emotion that you want to convey during each portion of the show.

Comedy it's all that matters

Comedy really is the core of the most modern day hypnosis shows and you will need comedy within your show. Luckily this is easily created by having your volunteers do silly things.

When it comes to comedy it's all about the people and situations that they normally be in and adding a silly twist. For instance if you take the beach skit and you have them imagine the sun shining down and they put sunscreen on their nose, ears, toes, elbows, and then finally there butt it becomes hilarious with each new thing that you get them to do. Comedy has a lot to do with the art building up to a joke into a climax.

When you're thinking through your skits I would suggest that you think them through from the least comedy value within that skit to the highest comedy value in sequence your skit that way. This creates a natural climax to your skits. From there are of course you can transition into another skit or simply put them back under for a little break as you prepare for your next skit sequence.

Drama it's all that matters

Every reality TV show is based on one simple thing drama, drama can be extremely entertaining if used in the right context.

When you're creating your skits one thing you should consider is thinking through how you can create more drama within them. One skit that I am able to create drama within is the movie skit. In that skit I get them to watch a happy movie that a sad movie then a romantic movie than a funny movie than a boring movie and then scary movie.

Throughout that skit sequence I am of course describing what's possibly happening in this movie and getting the audience involved and when the scary movie at the end is happening it becomes very dramatic as the audience becomes ghosts going boo, and werewolves howling while they watched the reactions of the people on stage. This skit all climaxes at the end of the music is playing when there's a scream.

The skit is a very dramatic skit and actually serves a purpose for the rest of my show because I make it a motivational skit. If I was just doing this skit to scare people it would still work however it may not go over as well with my audiences and personally I like to give a little bit back during the show's so I use this skit to let them know that they can overcome almost anything in their lives provided they choose to do so and put in the hard work.

The final portion of this skit ends with me playing triumphant superman style music and letting them know that they are just as good as anyone else and deserve to live the life that they choose.

What can you do in your chosen skits that can provide a motivational moment? What about inspiration, what about a cringe, what about a scare? It is all drama when played right.

Drama can sometimes create a very emotional experience, but also a very motivational one as well. Use it wisely!

Thrill is all that matters

The thrill the thrill the thrill Sunday, Sunday, Sunday…. Monster trucks live at your show. Yep your show can be absolutely thrilling, how do you create that thrill well make them do thrilling things.

Driving a car superfast on the highway, flying in a spaceship, watching an action movie, all of these can be extremely thrilling so use that your advantage.

Think up at least one skit through your show that you know will be extremely thrilling. It should take as much out of your audience as it does you and your volunteers.

I want you to take those audience members on the ride of their life. After my show is over the night is over because they are ready for bed. The point is to give them an experience and make it count. When someone asks them how the show was or if they know a hypnotist make sure they say: I saw the _____ show get him because he is the best!

Motivation it's all that matters

I'm a big time believer in the power of motivation during a hypnosis show. Why? Because when I was first hypnotized the hypnotist gave me some motivation during the show that actually played a major role in my life.

With hypnosis whether you believe in it or not doesn't matter, it's what your subjects believe. With a strong enough belief your subjects could accomplish anything they so desired which is why I highly suggest figuring out for yourself different ways to motivate people during your show.

Creating a motivational show will set you apart from others specifically if you use storytelling during your show.
There are other ways to set yourself apart so why not think of some and maybe you can be the next famous hypnotist.

The story is all that matters

For me the story does matter it's how I format my show and it's the type of show that I like. It's my personal belief the next generation of great entertainers will be the ones they can tell the best stories. It doesn't matter if your juggler a magician clown hypnotist speaker or Billy the stilt walker if you can tell a good story with the emotional impact that teaches your audience something or gives them hope you will be the next famous person in your field. Personally I am a midrange storyteller and I have got better as time moved on.

Storytelling isn't just about the story of the show it's also about your personal story as well. If you can mix your personal stories of triumph or adversity into the show through skits and comedy you will be remembered.

We can all watch a comedy hypnosis show the problem though is that 99% of them are all the same there's nothing to differentiate them the easiest way is through telling your story. It's also the hardest way because you have to give something of yourself to the audience and be vulnerable.

When you put love forth into the world it comes back to you and if one person doesn't like your story who cares you reach 99% of the rest of the audience. That 99% will remember you for ever if your story is formatted correctly here's a quick exercise that will help you figure out a small portion of your story.

It may sound like hippy dippy bull manure but it is true!

Exercise: Write your story

Grab a pen and a blank piece of paper. Grab a clock or your phone or your oven timer and set it for seven minutes. Now think of one incident in your life where you overcame adversity. Hit start on the timer and write for the next seven minutes about what you felt thought did and how you personally changed during this time period So you could overcome that adversity. Go do this exercise right now.

All done? Good it wasn't that hard right! Now go back and do it one more time.

Perfect, now think about how you could work even one sentence about this experience into your show. A show with a message of triumph can be sold to many different markets if formatted and performed correctly.

This in my opinion is one of the big keys to attaining the next level in your show. The story you tell does not matter other than it must be personal to you and you must believe the message you are sending.

IT ALL MATTERS!

Everything we've talked about action comedy motivation drama thrill story it all matters. You don't have to have every one of those elements in every show but if you do it creates a more complete entertainment experience. During your show you're going to have peaks and valleys climaxes and boring parts and that's all part of the show. Without these things your show could languish and not be as good as it could be.

It is your job as an entertainer to entertain, as a performer to perform, so do it go out there format your show properly. Look at it as if you were going to go and do a Broadway play practised 1000 times rewritten 100 times directed from blood sweat and tears.

Go into your show become your show then and only then will you begin to have a great show. This will take time you do not have to have all of this in place in your first show. You won't have in place by your 10th show or your 100th show even me the guy writing a book on the subject I'm still refining mine and will be until I stop doing

133

shows. It is a continual process and all the great ones do it so do it too. Refine and test refine and test.

It is okay, the whole point of this section is to make you think about what goes into good entertainment. If we don't think things through we can never improve as an industry which is what we are. The stage hypnosis industry.

We are the stage hypnosis industry and when you think about it very little is changed over the years people have been performing the same style of show with the skits that they've stole from other people and not making it their own with their own personality. It's my firm belief that that is why there's never been a major television show featuring stage hypnosis that was actually a hit.

You look at other forms of writing entertainment from singers to magicians to ventriloquists and they have all had hit shows in their industry while the hypnosis industry really has had nothing. The difference was and is that those other entertainment subsets bring one important factor and that is their personality and their story.

Small town chamber of commerce yes I can do that!

A show can even be good when you only keep a few STARS! It happens to every one eventually!

A picture of a bunch of ladies racing cars!

Chapter 8 Your Closing of the show

There are a lot of different skits that you can use at the end of your show as your big finish, from dancing, to see naked people, to anything else. The way I choose to end the show is using Richard Cole's 18 K skit as a post hypnotic suggestion you can find at 18Kskit.com it is a great little piece that makes sure people in your audience remember your name for a long time. This is a great way to get more business as you are the first person they think of when it comes to a hypnotist. I use it before my closing but a lot of people like to close with it and use it as a post hypnotic.

Ending with motivation

In my show I always end no matter what with some motivation whether it is whenever they see their favourite colour they'll be more confident in their life, or allowing them to imagine achieving their goals, or just giving them the confidence to move forward with the dreams they have. This all is part of my hypnosis show no matter what market I'm working from bars all the way to corporate and the reason is because it differentiates me from just the guy doing silly stuff. I would recommend to you that you create your own motivational skit as a show closer and use that.

If you're interested in the specifics of how I close my show I put out a product with Geoff Ronning a long time ago called dreams coming true if you like it it's available for purchase from the stagehypnosiscentre.com/store along with a bunch of other great products from Geoff.

Bringing them out of hypnosis

It's important that you bring people out in a proper way removing all suggestions and leaving them feeling fantastic. Generally I will close my show like this.

"Ladies and gentlemen thank you for coming here tonight in a few moments I will bring them out of hypnosis but before I do that in a few moments they're going to become very very confident in themselves more confident than they've ever been this suggestion will follow them through life.

Remember ladies and gentlemen that tonight we did record the entire show so if you would like a DVD copy of that please meet me over at that table right there and we will send one out to you.

We also have available several of my motivational CDs that have helped countless people across the country from stop smoking weight loss pain control insomnia and stress we have CDs available for you. CDs and DVDs are $35 each so please when the show is over make your way to the table right over there. And now back to the show.

Every suggestion I have given they will remember however they no longer react to any of them. From this point forward they will remember the whole show what they did and they won't be embarrassed in any way shape or form except these next ones..

This is where I would insert Richard Coles 18K skit!

When I count from 1 to 5 they will come completely and totally out of hypnosis when they do they will feel refreshed relaxed and at ease as if they've had eight hours of sleep and they're ready to just have some more fun 1 coming out just a little wee bit 2 coming out just a little wee bit more 3 feeling revitalized refreshed taking in a deep breath and allowing your temperature and body functions to return to normal in a few moments you will come out of hypnosis to a wonderful standing ovation because you have done one heck a show for this audience get ready everyone to give these volunteers some applause 4 be coming completely and totally relaxed feeling refreshed and 5 if your eyes are not already eyes open wide they can open now wide awake remembering everything right now give them a big round of applause"

This makes it so they feel good once they're done the show getting a round of applause at the end is exhilarating and it's important that you give it to your volunteers. You know you did all the hard work but it was their imagination that made the show possible so give them thanks.

It is also great to catch on camera at a few shows and put it into your demo DVD with you and the audience in the background!

At this point you will generally find me saying thank you one more time and letting them know that I'll be back at the BOR table where they can purchase copies of the show or motivational hypnosis CDs DVDs and most recently instant digital downloads to their phones or computers.

This is how I bring my show to a close and ensure that my volunteers feel good afterwards. Sometimes after the show you may get somebody who says they think they're stuck in hypnosis. While you and I know that this is impossible the general population isn't that bright sometimes. Sometimes they even panic because they feel weird compared to how they felt before the show.

This can generally be attributed to the release of stress when they relax and let themselves go. A hypnosis show can actually be a very emotional experience for some people. If someone comes to you and says I feel like I'm stuck in hypnosis or they say my friend is still hypnotized you need to deal with this promptly and effectively.

My solution is to simply stated that a person cannot get stuck in hypnosis and if a person feels weird after the show it's generally because they allow themselves to relax a lot and that the show was a very active show so they may not be used to all the action that was happening on stage.

Let them know it's impossible to get stuck in hypnosis because hypnosis is an everyday state of life and even if they were stuck they would come out within about a minute and a half of not hearing the hypnotist. When a person is hypnotized they follow directions therefore if they were hypnotized and followed directions then that means when the hypnotist says you will come out of hypnosis they will come out of hypnosis.

This is a wonderful Catch-22 for your volunteers and in fact sometimes I add it into the show by saying it's impossible to get stuck in hypnosis's on the count of three you will come out of hypnosis on the count of five you will come out of hypnosis because if you didn't we all know that you're just trying to get attention because people in hypnosis follow directions.

This is really a good practice sometimes as there will be people pretending to be in hypnosis through the whole show. Or they may not understand how easy it is to come out. I am there to entertain not be a baby sitter. I include this in the book because a few years ago there was a hypnotist in Montreal at a school that caused a national news story when he could not get a girl out of hypnosis. Bad training and bad learning can lead to bad results for the whole industry.

It is important that you understand this aspect of people thinking they've is stuck in hypnosis. If a hypnotist lets people think they're stuck or does not deal with this properly it gives the whole business a bad name and the next time that that group or that entire audience if they saw what went down sees a hypnosis show they could be afraid to go into hypnosis.

People are not as smart as they should be and they are smarter than we ever thought possible too. Please make sure that you remember this portion of the book bring them out properly and don't let anybody pretend that they're stuck in hypnosis because that's just bullshit.

Multimedia can be fun during a hypnosis show to add some flair! Yes that is an elephant balancing on a ball back there!

Chapter 9 THE FUN HOME WORK CHAPTER.

This whole book has been about you developing your own unique style in your own unique show but in this chapter I want you to go back to something that you may not of been able to do for yourself yet and that is the show evaluation.

There are many examples of hypnosis shows on YouTube and I would like you to watch them. Hypnosis shows on-screen are generally not very entertaining because it's more of a personal aspect that makes the shows more entertaining. That's another part of the reason why we've never really had a hit TV series of hypnosis shows. If you want to go get one do it and make hypnosis become an even bigger player on the world stage. However this is designed to help you improve your fledgling show and make it better. I would like you to dissect a whole bunch of different hypnosis shows. Grab your computer and create this form:

Show Evaluation Form:

Show Date_____ Show Time _____

Venue _____

What was the reaction to your walk out and introduction? Where can it improve?

_____

_____

What was the reaction to your Pretalk? Where can it improve?

What was the reaction to your Routines?

_____

_____

_____

_____

_____

_____

_____

Post hypnotics

_____

_____

Were there new routines

_____

_____

List the biggest reactions during the show and review their wording

_____

_____

_____

_____

List the least reaction and review their wording

_____

_____

_____

What areas do you need to work on to improve the show next time.

_____

_____

_____

List three things you will improve and practice before your next performance

1. _____

2. _____

3. _____

Print ten of them out!

Now head over to you tube and find 10 full stage hypnosis shows that you can watch. Including pretalk and induction. It is important that you do not steal these people shows or material. These are refined shows that have taken these people years to develop. You don't want people stealing your stuff do not steal theirs. I would suggest you pick 10 shows from 10 different venues, fairs, bars, corporate, casino, college, schools, grads, find them and evaluate.

Most hypnosis trainers will have a full video online that you can view. There are two prominent Vegas stage hypnotists that have their full show online for sure so look for those two and find 3 to 5 other hypnosis shows that you can view online as well. This will give you a good understanding of what actually goes into a hypnosis show. If you have someone you admire in the business see if they have their full show online.

My full show is floating around out there somewhere and it gets updated every once in a while so if you want to see it just look up show video for Jesse Lewis full show and you should be able to find it quickly

What to study about these shows? – structure, pre-talk and induction length, skits, laughter, drama, Motivational bits and anything else that you are interested in for your stage hypnosis show. This is designed for you to get an understanding of how to actually do a show evaluation. Do not steal their shows it will not come off well and if you do well you're an idiot and the thief.

Have fun and enjoy your next 15 hours of watching YouTube videos.

When you are done I bet that you have found a bunch of ways to improve their show and format yours more effectively too.

Chapter 10: Setting the stage

Sound is a major component of the hypnosis show. You need it for several reasons.

1. To be louder than your audience so they can hear you clearly.

2. So the volunteers can hear you clearly.

I prefer to carry my own sound to most shows just in case. This can be an issue for many beginning performers but it should not be. If you have a chance see if your venue has a suitable sound system and test it long before the show. If it is not suitable rent one from Long and Mcquade in Canada or Guitar Center in the USA or any other sound rental company out there.

Generally for a quality sound system I pay under $100 per month to rent. You will need a sound system suitable for your venue and a microphone that you like using.

I recommend using a handheld mic but also don't mind the headset ones. A lavaliere microphone is a big no for me as that type often has rubbing sounds if you are moving around on stage.

If you are running music you will also need an input device and cord like a laptop or iPhone or iPod or MP3 player or whatever sound device you're going to be using to play in control your music. I use a laptop running Winamp and a PowerPoint presenter remote. It's cheap and effective I was up and running for approximately $13 because I already own the laptop.

When it comes to sound equipment I would highly suggest that you rent a few different models before you ever purchase one. Every type of sound equipment has a different sound, quality, and control system. The current sound equipment I'm using in my show is the

Yamaha Stagepass 500. I have worked with groups up to 700 in a school gymnasium and that system worked wonderfully.

For many larger shows I require them to provide sound that is suitable for the venue right in my contract.

Microphones

For me I prefer Sennheiser mics as they give a better quality of sound with my voice. Many other performers prefer Shure mics. For me I require a wireless mic because I move around a lot and I like to have more interaction with my volunteers. Not having a cord following you around just looks better in general.

Testing Testing 123

That's right its sound check time and there is a very important way that you are going to perform your sound checks. There is nothing worse than having your sound not suitable for the venue either to high-pitched to low-pitch dead in some areas or just plain awful. Bad sound can ruin show faster than you ever thought possible. Don't let your sound be crappy because it's really your butt on the line.

Here's how I perform a sound check.

Mindset of the sound check:

1. If you're lucky enough to have a sound tech get to know them shake their hand and remember their name. They are your ally.
2. Figure out where your house (venue) and stage lights switches and how you are going to want them set for Showtime. Memorize or create a diagram for exactly how you want them set. (Someone will mess with them.)

3. Understand that you are the entertainer and sound of your show depends on you. If you trust others to set your sound up chances are you will sound like crap.

Actual sound check

1. Arrive at your venue early so you can plan set up and test your sound and lights before anyone gets there.
2. Once sound is set up speak softly and then loudly into the microphone
3. Move around the stage and check for feedback problems
4. Move around the room as much as possible and check for feedback and dead spots
5. If you plan on going into the audience during the show at all for any skits you must also do a sound check in the seating area.
6. Do you use music? Run through it each and every cue to make sure it is working. Nothing is worse than saying on the count of three you will hear banjos and all that plays is silence.
7. You need to listen to what's actually coming out of the speakers at every point in the room. Front and back sides all of it because during the show you will be talking in different volume levels and now is the time to learn if your soft phrases will be clearly heard and if you're loud voice will come through clearly.

If you do not have a wireless microphone get someone to stand on stage and talk while you go to all parts of the room and listen to what you have available.

The last thing I'm going to suggest you with in regards to sound is to use a handheld microphone. The reason being is that it gives you far greater control over your voice than any other type. It allows you to move it in and away from your mouth and get volunteer reactions on the microphone as well. This is an important aspect of the hypnosis show as the show really is about them and what they're doing.

It's important your record each every show you perform so you have a record of what happened during the show. This serves two purposes first is that you can improve your show by re-watching the old videos and second it can help you if you ever have a lawsuit against you to prove whether you're right or wrong. The cameras I prefer for stage work are cannons. They seem to record better quality than the competition and I'm satisfied with what I get. When I record I use a camera that's capable of high definition recording.

By this point you're probably wondering how to set the actual stage in the following pages I will give different ways that I have set the stage and what works for me as well is some examples of what not to do so that you have a good working area on stage.

Stage set up one: my preferred setup with two speakers:

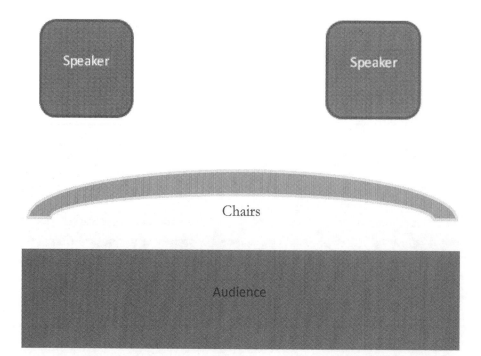

This setup is for when you have only two speakers and accomplishes two things.

1. It allows for good sound on the stage.

2. It allows for good sound in the audience.

Sometimes with this configuration I will cross the speakers to create a better sound quality for the audience getting rid of dead spots. With all configurations for the speakers I would suggest you check thoroughly for feedback and adjust accordingly to get the best quality of sound.

Prefered setup 2

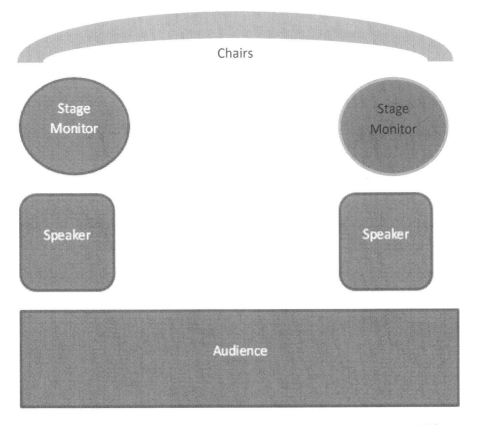

In this configuration you have two stage monitors that point directly at the chairs and two speakers that point out towards the audience. This gives much better control over your sound in general but can also be a much bigger hassle to set-up. This is the general configuration you should ask for if you will be performing in a theater or venue that will be providing you with sound. In my experience it also helps with the actual hypnotising process as it cuts down a lot of the back ground noise and minimizes distractions.

Controlling your music:

The cheap way:

The cheapest possible way to control your music is to not have music to begin with however music really can make the show pop. When I first started I actually controlled all of my music from a portable DVD player. It cost me about 60 bucks and I had a track list printed out beside it. This allowed me to know what track was going to play so didn't have any missed sound cues. It also kept me stationary during the show as I had to be right beside the sound. If I was smarter I would of course used the remote. For bar shows and low end shows it worked fine.

The Easy Way

Do you have a laptop? Is it PC-based? Do you have the ability to download Win-amp? Do you have the ability to spend $17 on Amazon for a PowerPoint remote? If you answered yes to these questions you have the basics of a remote-controlled sound system.

This is what I personally use and I find it absolutely amazing for controlling my sound. I bought a cheap remote and just use Winamp. In Winamp's preferences allows me to make the text any size I need to be to see my playlist and with the remote I can switch seamlessly between songs. It takes a little bit of you getting used to the system but it is just as good as many of more expensive systems out there. Richard Cole is the one that originally introduced me to the system and I would never go back to using a different way. He has an awesome tutorial on how to set it up in detail so hit him up for more information!

The expensive way

There are many fancy gizmos out there for your sound but they'll basically work on same principle as the easy way to explained above. They're all basically remote systems. If you don't want a remote based sound system I would suggest hiring a sound person.

Hiring a sound person is by far the most expensive way to do sound for your show however it is also the best option for many entertainers as it gives them the freedom to do whatever else that they need to do. For me personally I do not like having a sound person as I would rather cue the music myself and have control. This makes it so there's no one else to blame but myself during the show.

Chapter 11: Markets for your show

There are literally hundreds of markets for your shelf incorporate to cruises to bars to schools and every other market in between a hypnosis show is very versatile and can fit in almost anywhere.

Low hanging fruit

Bars, hotels, restaurants, banquet halls, senior centres, service clubs, and other venues like this are considered low hanging fruit and should be relatively easy to book.

Cream of the crop

Corporate, Casinos, Large fairs, Colleges, Theaters. This is the place to make money but you have to be dam good. Experience matters but not that much. Here is an article I wrote about paying your dues for my website – showbizsuccesssecrets.com

Booking your first shows

- Fast booking strategy the art of the door deal

This is the 30 Day Hypnosis Business Builder do it and make it work for you!

The door deal is old as the hills and can be used anywhere. It has literally built businesses and can give you one hell of a steady income when used properly. There are two main advantages of the door deal when you first start out:

1. you get paid to learn your art

2. You get paid to learn how to promote your show.

The venues

Bars, Restaurants, banquet halls and other places that are already doing events that may have a slow night or unused space.

The one thing you have to do to find success is:

DO THE FREAKING WORK you hurt no one but yourself if you do not.

Turn the TV off for the next thirty days and use those hours to book shows or work on your business.

Fast Start Strategies

There is one basic fast start strategy we will use throughout this program. The "bar" booking strategy. We will use this to book more than just bars and learn how to use it effectively long term.

Mindset

If you think this will not work you are right you have to believe it will work and you will have success. One no does not mean all no's. Someone will say yes and that is when your real work begins.

You should expect to book the gig when you walk in. If you truly expect to book the gig you probably will. The fact is these people need you to be more profitable so let them know about you.

Why the bar booking strategy? Because they are easy bookings when first starting out. They can be stacked up like cord wood (If you get that reference awesome.) They teach you more than any other type of show.

The Bar Booking Strategy Identifying prospects

Identifying your prospects is the first step and there are some main criteria that I use when I do the bar booking strategy.

1. The show must be at least one month away
2. They must have the ability to make money other than the door. IE: FOOD OR DRINKS
3. They must have an off night where they are slow and you can bring in guests.

There is a huge opportunity in these venues for you to affect their bottom line and yours as well. It is your job to offer them a show. You keep the ticket sales and they keep the food. If you do not bring people in you do not get paid.

You should be able to find these venues in two ways

Physically go to them or go Online – use business directories for your local communities, Google, and anything else you can think of to just find them.

Another thing you can look for is "associations for these types of venues, hotels association, catering association, that type of thing. If you do find an assosication for this type iof venue you have just created your first list! Awesome. Put these into a spread sheet that will be important later.

Your approach:

Go to the venue.

Ask for the owner or whoever is in charge of the space.

Ask them if they would be open to having you come in and do entertainment for the door admission. You keep the door and they keep the food and drinks you take the ticket sales.

They will say yes or no

If they say no walk across the street and offer their competition the same deal…. And keep going until you book a show. When I first started it took me 30 tries to get a door deal. Now I get it almost every time. It is all about confidence.

If they say yes: Ask them for a date 1 month away so you can promote the living heck out of it. Get them to sign a performance agreement with the details of what will be done by both parties and you are good to go.

How you profit:

You charge minimum of $5 - $10 at the door per person.

If you do not bring any one in you make no money welcome to show business.

You sell BOR at shows:

You do have your BOR ready don't you? Don't worry there is a section later that explains all about passive income and BOR dollars.

You build a list over time which you can promote to later (upcoming shows, new BOR products)

You rebook the shows over and over and book other shows off of them as well (If and when you do a good job)

How they profit:

They sell food and drinks and have a crowd brought to them by you.

They have quality entertainment that they do not have to do anything to promote!

What about objections

"WELL WILL I HAVE TO PROMOTE THE SHOW…"

They can if they choose but let them know you will promote for free. Press releases, Posters, table tents, social media everything you can possibly do to make it a success.

"WHAT IF NO ONE SHOWS UP"

Well that means you will pay me nothing at all and I show up and probably have a meal or a few drinks with you.

Start this process today. There is no reason you cannot book up as many of these that you want. Just go out and do it quit being a wimp and get off your butt make your dream come true. You are not going to get where you want to go without the hard work involved in getting there.

"WHY ARE YOU DOING THIS"

To get my name out there locally and have some fun. I want to help you make more money for your business it is as simple as that.

What it the manager is not there:

Ask when they will be back and follow up at that time.

Get the places email and biz card. I will reveal a strategy to possibly book later. These are valuable contacts no matter what people tell you and you can make money from and for them.

SO HERE IS A SCRIPT YOU CAN PRACTICE WITH SOMEONE TO GET USED TO THE PROCESS:

The process and presentation of booking low hanging fruit:

The first person you hypnotize is yourself.

Process:

- Have the intention of knowing you will book them.
- Approach them
- Offer "free to them" show for the DOOR admission or a percentage of it.
- Let them know you will promote for free, posters, table tents, everything.

The Presentation for booking shows:

You: "Hey you the owner"

Them: Yes I am

You: "My name is ____ I have an idea that I think can bring in some more people do you mind if I share it with you."

Them: Sure

You: "I'm a comedy stage hypnotist and I just moved to this area and I think if I came in on a Thursday like last night, helped promote the show, we could pack in more people and they would spend more money. I would be willing to do it for the door how does that sound."

Them: Ya Sure

You: "What do you want from me right now or should we just try it. "

Them: Let's look at my calendar and we will pencil you in for next Thursday

You: "Awesome and if this works out we could do it on a regular basis"

Them: I would be willing to give you a shot, what were you thinking for a door split

You: "What do you want to charge for tickets"

Them: For a Thursday 8 bucks

You: "How about I take 80% you take 20% and you keep all the food and beverage sales. "

Them: I would be willing to give it a shot at that, and if no one shows I don't pay anything

You: Awesome lets pencil it in I will start promoting right away.

HOME WORK

I want you to make a list of 100 possible venues and over the next week visit 25 venues minimum or until you book 3 shows. Do this NOW and book a freaking show. Even in very low population areas you can do this. It is not just bars it is restaurants, service clubs, hotels, and any other place that has events or an empty room in which you can perform. If people say no just move on it is not the end of the world. I have had people say no to me and then a year later they called me to book. They paid my full price too.

If you book more than 3 shows from those 25 visits awesome. If you are having trouble finding venues here is a more extensive list of who may be interested and where to find them:

- In The Newspaper -> places that already have/host events
- ON The Internet -> Places already having events
- City business directories
- Associations -> catering, hotels, hospitality
- Physically ->By going to places and looking around

- Tourism Mags

What types of venues you want to look for:

- Bars, taverns, pubs
- Restaurant
- Banquet halls
- Comedy clubs
- Dance halls
- Bingo halls
- Community theaters
- Community Halls
- Concert halls
- Golf Clubs
- Meeting Hotels with unused banquet space
- Museums
- Resorts
- Sports arena's , hockey, curling, baseball
- Service Clubs

Chapter 12 Promoting Public shows

If you are doing public shows learning how to promote them effectively is actually harder than learning stage hypnosis! Let's go over the basics of promotion in todays markets.

POSTERS

Ask any carnival front man and he will tell you posters are essential so make them and use them! Below are a few examples of posters that I have used in the past:

LIVE IN THE BROOKSBY HALL MAY 9TH

PLUS FIVE 5 ENTERTAINMENT PRESENTS

THE OFF THE HOOK HYPNOSIS SHOW

A Night In LAS VEGAS

Vegas Style Buffet Meal,

The Off the Hook Hypnosis Show With Jesse Lewis

DJ and Dance, Door Prizes, Raffles

Tickets are available Book your table now!

Elvis Will Be There To Renew Your Vows

Get your Tickets from Plus 5 Entertainment

NOW: Call 1-306-276-9433

GET HYPNOTIZED

THE JESSE LEWIS HYPNOSIS SHOW

see The Show OR Be The Show!

The real key to a good poster is to get attention. The following is a basic guide to poster creation that will help immensely if you are just starting out with posters

Posters should be:

- Easy to understand from across the room
- Eye Catching
- Be Brief
- Be Cheap
- Focused on the event not your ego
- Use Hypnotic Language
- Give information about the show (happy hour, supper, other stuff)

Posters are a numbers game:

- The more you put up the more people see them.
- The more people see them the more tickets you will sell
- The more tickets you sell the more you make

Figure out as many places in your area that you possibly can to put posters up.

Poster Components:

Headline:

- Name of the show
- Make sure HYPNOSIS is prominent in name

We are no name headliners we rely on the "show" not our names to make sales. Use the knowledge that the show is the sale maker at this point not you.

Your Graphics:

- Nice and eye catching
- Not too large
- Large enough to be seen from a distance

Graphics are easy to find and purchase these days and if you are making a generic long use poster which will be reusable over time you need to have a blank space at the bottom for the potential client to fill information in.

Currently I am using an online service called Canva for any new poster I make. It costs $1 per image I use of theirs and allows me to design some very nice posters for my public events.

The next part of the poster is the Performers Name:

- Smaller
- No one cares about you but that does not matter sell the tickets not "YOU"

Venue:

- Medium size
- Address
- Phone number

Ticket Price:

- Medium font
- usually under venue

Date:

- Second largest font next to headline

Misc Stuff:

- Back by popular demand
- Some skits you perform
- Tagline
- Indication of show content (adult, clean, Dancing with monkeys)
- Show benefits
- ETC
- In this package you received three posters you can modify to your needs.

With posters:

- Less is often more
- You are not trying to win a design award keep it simple and readable
- Sometimes fancy text is harder to read

Paper size:

For low hanging fruit bookings I use legal paper size which is basically longer paper. It is easy to mail for long distance gigs and easy to have on hand for putting up. As well most home printers these days can print legal size if you are in "remote" areas like me 2 hours from the nearest printer.

Where to get them printed:

- Kinko's staples or other short run printers is fine
- All of mine are printed at home

Quantity to place:

I print a minimum of 25 per venue and put all of them up. The more the better; if you are in an area that you can place more do so. It will get your numbers up and the better the numbers the more profit you will have.

Of course these are just general rules for the posters and you can make yours any way you wish. The most important thing is to really get them out there in advance of the show.

Table tents

Table tents are the little stands you see at restaurants that promote specials or events that are coming to the venue. These are a great way to promote an are very easy to make.

The same rules apply for table tents as posters in regards to the design in fact when I make table tents it really is just a smaller version of my posters. Some good things to put on table tents are myths about hypnosis, where to but tickets, price, a picture or anything else you think is suitable. Below is one of my table tent designs.

GET

HYPNOTIZED!!!!

The Jesse Lewis Comedy Hypnosis Show

This Place Thursday August 8th 10 PM

Get Your Tickets Today

Five Big Myths About Hypnosis

1. Hypnosis is sleep?

No it is not during hypnosis you are even more awake than you are right now just really focused

2. I won't remember anything!

After the show you will remember everything you do.

3. The hypnotist is funny looking!

Ok this is not a myth He is but that's ok you gotta be weird to do this job.

4. I will lose all control!

No during hypnosis you will be fully aware you just will not care as long as the suggestions are not against your morals you will follow them.

5. I cannot be hypnotised!

Only those who truly do not want to be hypnotised cannot be. Hypnosis is not some magical force it is a science anyone can learn and do. It has been used in medicine for years and the only person who cannot get hypnotised is someone who truly does not want to

Press releases

Publicity:

Getting publicity adds credibility to your business whether newspaper, TV, or radio publicity it is great.

You can use publicity to bulk up your promotional package, sell bor, and prove you are a great choice for entertainment. Many entertainers do not understand the power of publicity and are confused with how to actually put it to good use.

If what you are given here is not enough for you go to shobizsuccesssecrets.com and pick up Publicity for performers it is the most in depth training out there for entertainers to get press and yes I created it.

Publicity 101:

- **Most publicity is placed**
- **Submit press releases for own exposure**
- **Publicity should be a constant marketing because -1. Its free and 2. It establishes credibility with your clients.**
- **You can be your own PR guy or Gal**
- **Always submit press releases**
- **Template Articles**

An easy way to do this is to have template articles premade into which you just insert the show information. This makes it easy to produce the press releases and keeps your workload down.

Creating a press release:

There are five basic questions that should be answered by any press release:

- WHAT
- WHO
- WHY
- WHERE
- WHEN

A press release should be formatted in a very specific way or maximum effect. Below are tips on formatting any press release. These tips are general rules for submitting press releases for any media outlet.

Dos and Don'ts of Press releases:

Dos

- Give your press release a date
- Give it a snappy headline that tells the story in brief.
- Type it but keep it short, simple and preferably on a single sheet. Use approximately three sentences per paragraph. Double space the entire release so it's easier to read.
- Number the pages; end the first with 'more follows'; start the second with a new paragraph; on the final page finish off with 'ends'.
- Try to get all the crucial information in the opening paragraph or two - including who, what, when, where, why/how.
- Include an interesting 'quote' from an identified spokesperson. This may be you or if you have permission the event organiser.
- Provide contact name/s and 'phone number/s - make sure all your key people have a copy, and that at you are available outside office hours (with a copy of the release and any useful background information)
- Always give details of what, when and where photographs can be taken.
- Add brief extra background information in a 'Notes to Editors' section if necessary.
- Check deadlines in advance - make sure your release arrives in time for journalists to follow it up.

- When possible follow up with a phone call - if it hasn't been received, send over another copy at once.

DO NOTS

- Never assume the reader will know all about your story or what you do.
- Rambling prose and irrelevant crap detract from the impact of your story.
- Don't include irrelevant details keep to the important points. If the journalist wants to expand on your story they will call you or research you themselves.
- Avoid repetition, clichés, jargon, and abbreviations. Don't try to write the journalist's headline for them with clever puns just tell the facts simply.
- Never make claims you cannot prove, and avoid exaggeration - overstating your case is more likely to wreck than to win you an interview.
- Sloppy presentation, mistakes and bad grammar damage credibility - get someone to check for grammar, whether it makes sense, accuracy, and spelling.
- Ignore media interest in your press release at your peril - you sought their attention, so return their calls. Otherwise you can end up with a bad story about you.

General format for a press release

Heading:

The heading should be typed in bold and centred. Keep it short, snappy and to the point.

First paragraph:

Start with a bang. Get the five W's in straight away Who, When, What, Where, Why.

Following paragraphs:

Make your points in order of importance. The second paragraph should elaborate on the first one. You are essentially telling a story, so you must give the reader the full picture. Spell out the facts, give statistics, quote names and numbers of people involved.

Quotes:

Include a direct quote from the most relevant person involved, it will humanise the story. Keep the quote brief, providing an overview of the event. If writing a quote for somebody else, get their approval before using it. Remember to give the person's full name and job title.

More follows...

If the press release goes onto a second page, type "more follows" at the bottom right hand corner and "continued" at the top of the second page. Never split paragraphs or sentences.

ENDS or ####

Make sure it is clear where your story ends.

Contact: Give names and telephone numbers of people a journalist can contact for further information.

Notes to Editors: This is your last chance to give journalists details of how they can get copies of a report, photograph or any other information.

A sample press release follows on the next page feel free to modify and use it for your purposes.

For Immediate Release

June 06 2013

Hypnotizing For Horses

David's Lizard Lounge will be jumping with fun, laughter and definite foolishness as Master Hypnotist Jesse Lewis excites the audience with his hilarious hypnosis show on July 20th, 2013 at David's Lizard Lounge with a show that is sure to sell out.

During the show ordinarily conservative audience members and even those who aren't so conservative will undergo a complete transformation. The actions that Jesse puts them through are hilarious to the audience members, but to the volunteers up on stage it becomes their reality. Of course, the show is all great fun and will have the audience laughing non-stop from start to finish during this special appearance.

Jesse Lewis, a graduate of The Hypnosis Motivation Institute, told us, "I'm excited with the opportunity of presenting my Comedy Hypnosis show to raise funds for this great cause! People can often help themselves but animals are sometimes stuck in horrible situations and need help. I am just doing my part to help Paradise Stable Horse Rescue. The Show will be exciting and will involve a number of audience members! The individuals who volunteer for the show are the ones who will have the most fun."

The Jesse Lewis Hypnosis show has been seen all over western Canada for the past five years and crowds everywhere have enjoyed the show.

"I hope to see everyone at the show, and, oh yes it is for real. If you have any doubts, join us and volunteer see what happens. Even if you do not volunteer you can still have a lot of fun and raise money for the stables!"

The show is to raise funds for the paradise Stable Horse rescue based out of Saskatoon. The Horse Rescue is dedicated to giving horses a second chance.

Tickets available at _____

For more information contact Jesse Lewis at 1-888-XXX-XXXX or email _____ For a quote from paradise stables contact Bunnie at 1-306-XXX-XXXX

That is a standard press release that I have reformatted for many shows and has been printed verbatim in several papers.

It contains all of the strong points of any press release and because it is for a good cause it got picked up and ran in two newspapers one weekly and one daily. It has been profitable for my promotional package and my bank account.

Where and how to send press releases.

Build another list: Of all of the media contacts in your area. Radio, TV, Newspaper, no matter how large or how small.

This can be done two ways look them up online or look them up in the phone book or business directories. Get their mailing address fax and phone numbers if possible. Some libraries have free media directories if so use them.

I have a set calendar for submitting press releases as follows:

1-month out- send press release by fax

2-weeks out send press release by mail

1-week out send press release by fax and email call to make sure they received it

1 week after send press release about previous event with pictures if possible. This sometimes will get you more exposure even after the event.

Send to all media outlets TV RADIO AND NEWSPAPER

Contacts are put into a database

Other options for getting continual media exposure are:

- Become a weekly or monthly guest columnist
- It's easy free and establishes you as an expert

Easy topics are entertainment, event planning, fundraising, or anything to do with hypnosis. These can then go into your promotional package. These may or may not be paid positions but the point is to promote.

Stories that you submit do not necessarily have to have an event associated with them for instance when The Duchess Kate used hypnosis for childbirth. That was a great way to have a tie in about what hypnosis is and the myths and misconceptions and all that jazz. If you submitted a press release during that time about hypnosis you were a smart cookie.

Facebook

My Facebook marketing approach is simple I post 3 posts per week per public event I have coming up. They get shared to the venue's page and to my fan page wall. On top of that I do a general promotion of a show video from the past that is a lot of fun.

Mailing list blasts

If you are just starting out you will not have a list but if you do you can also use do a blast to previous attendees. The easiest way to do this is to start collecting names and emails and do a monthly newsletter as a fan mail page. Dispel one myth talk about upcoming shows and give them something for free. Get people's information by creating a sheet for collecting information that they can sign up for to receive free stuff .

A method for getting awesome testimonials and building your list:

Place cards on all of the places at tables during the show and ask for an opinion from the patron written down on the card.

Collect the card after the show and you will have some nice testimonials for your promotional package. If you ask them for mailing info if they want more information about you then you have also built your list. Many people will be afraid to ask for information and this is a way to collect names easily for future show promotions/sales.

Getting a weekly gig

If your show goes well and you think it would work approach them for a weekly or monthly show. Use the same deal as before you promote they reap the drinks and food. The simplest way to do this is to just ask!

Booking your next shows in almost any market

- Marketing made simple

The act of marketing and selling is giving people the solution to their problem. For instance service clubs do not want to do fundraisers they want to have funds given to them without the work. Schools don't want a motivational hypnosis show they want a solution to their motivation problem in their school. By giving the solution to the true problems of our clients you become a winner and so do they.

For you to get gigs you are going to have to learn to market by many different means. Do not rely on only one form of marketing in case it ever dries up. In My very first years I did only one type of marketing and that was direct mail. It got me to two 70,000 dollar years in a row and then it turned into a 20 thousand dollar year afterwards, Was it still effective yes but I went from a good income to nothing over night and it created hardships for my family so learn different forms of marketing. Marketing through many channels gives much more security than just one do this and see what works and what does not it is different for everyone. There are many ways to market:

- **Direct mail**

Direct mail is either sending a postcard letter or flyer to prospective clients and it does work very well. In fact this was a mainstay of my marketing for the first five years.

- **Phone**

Repeat after me the phone is your friend, the phone is your friend, I would suggest refining your phone skills to the point you can book a show easily on it.

There are lots of great books on the subject and I suggest you read all of them and take as many courses on phone sales as possible. It is quickly becoming my mainstay for marketing.

- **Email**

Email is tricky because if you spam people they simply will not answer so be careful to obey all of your local regional and national laws. Generally when I email people I ask them first if they are the right person and second if I can send them something! It works and if they respond No I am not right they will generally send you to the person who is.

- Personal contact

It is Ok to do a walk in just don't waste peoples time, go in make an impact and get out! When I do this I do a short two minute presentation and leave then with my business card and demo DVD.

- Networking and referrals from shows

Networking and referrals for shows can be a huge source of income. I would suggest to you that you create a pitch that you can use at the beginning and end of your shows that generates show referals.

As far as networking goes I would join as many groups in my area as possible and see which ones pay off the most. Attend the meetings and do the work and you are sure to find success.

One of my many market specific onesheets!

Chapter 12: Promotional materials

So your show is ready to kick butt, heck if you're like me you've already performed one or two by the time you to this part of the book. But there's one thing you're missing to book bigger and better shows – – you need a promotional package.

A promotional package is what separates you from the other entertainers trying to get booked. The more professional you can make it the more professional type shows you will be able book. In fact I would suggest having a promotional package for each different market you go into. This means having a different promotional package for schools, corporate, service clubs, and any other market you look at.

- **Physical VS Online**

there is a great debate whether you should have a physical promotional package or online promotional package. I would suggest you that you should have both as different clients will want different things. A physical promotional package has exactly the same stuff as an online promotional package.

- One sheet

This is basically a sales sheet that explains what you do and the benefits of working with you. It is only one page no longer. I suggest keeping it simple and to the point. A title, a fun picture of you, a picture of you with an audience, and the benefits of hiring you. That really is all you need for a one sheet. A good place get one sheets done is on fiverr.

- Bio

Your biography is all about you. Without being about you that is. Generally for each of my promotional packs I suit my bio to fit the market. If it's the fundraising market I talk about the charitable work and fundraising I've helped do for other groups. If it is the corporate market I talk about my charitable work and working in the corporate market.

All my bio includes is one clean sheet of paper with my photograph and a 300 word biography. The biography is generally more about the type of client and how I have worked with them than it is about me. Honestly the client doesn't really care about me or you they care about the results they're going to get when they hire us.

- Pictures

Generally with each promotional package I will send an 8 x 10 signed of me on stage performing or a head shot. I will also send a collage of other performances as well. This is just a proof builder letting them know you are the real deal!

- Demo video

If you haven't done a show yet you won't have a demo video, however if you performed then you should have started collecting footage already.

A demo video can be anywhere from 30 seconds to 30 minutes depending on the market you are going into. I offer two types of demo videos to the markets that I'm in. The first is the 2:30 minute video. This is basically only highlights and a voiceover of the benefits that I provide with my show. The second is my full show video specific to that market that I'm going into or an adjacent one. Generally my full show video is about 45 minutes long and jampacked with fun.

If you are looking at getting you demo professionally done let me know and I will send you towards someone who does a fantastic job! This is provided you have the footage.

- Testimonials

Testimonials are an awesome addition to your promotional package. There are three types good old testimonial letter, audio testimonials, and video testimonials. How you get them differs in several different ways.

Letter testimonials

The first way to get a letter testimonial is to ask for one after you've performed and follow-up with the client. This is also the least effective way to get a testimonial.

A much better way to get a testimonial letter is to write two or three yourself send them to the client after you've performed and ask them which one they would approve.

Your client does not have time to be writing you testimonial letters and this saves them a huge amount of time and gives you the testimonial that you want.

Audio Testimonials are easy to get in two different ways.

The first way to get an audio testimonial is to ask your broker directly after the event if they would be able to do a quick audio testimonial into your cellular phone. Generally they will do this without a problem. Simply download a voice recording app onto your phone and you have their testimonial.

The second way to get an audio testimonials to ask them to leave a recording on your voicemail. Then you simply record this onto another medium and you are set. Make sure you get a very good recording of it before you delete the message as you will never ever get it back if you don't.

Video testimonials

These work basically the same way as an audio testimonial except you must get them on site or you will never get one. You grab your phone you switch on the camera mode go over to video and ask if your client would be willing to give a quick video testimonial as a huge favour to you. Some clients are not willing to do this and that is okay as you can ask them for an audio or letter testimonial. I find that video testimonials are actually the most effective testimonial I can have as they are very hard to fake. Never ever fake a testimonial as it will come back and bite you right in the ass.

-       **Web site**

eight years ago when I first started websites were really not that important. Today has changed all of that. In my opinion if you do not have a working website with decent Seo or the use of ad words then chances are you're not going to get booked online. For inspiration on your website I'm not even going to tell you where to look as your website needs to be your own. My website as ugly as it is still generates traffic and books shows.

Chapter 13: BOR Sales or back of room sales

BOR is huge, if you aren't selling BOR you are really missing out on a huge potential for income. Some entertainer's make as much with BOR as they do off of the show. There are a few types of different BOR - show videos, books, seminar DVDs, seminar cds, USB drives and instant downloads. All of them make money and you should be using them to your full advantage to increase your income.

- **Show videos**

If I was just starting out this is where I would start with BOR products. Recording and selling show videos can be a great little money maker. Currently I sell my show videos anywhere from $30 all the way up to $50 depending on the venue. For schools assemblies I do not sell show DVD's as generally they will not want you to record. It's different for fundraisers though. When I originally started I used a cheap Fujifilm camera that I had to hit the record button on twice as it would timeout after 30 minutes of recorded video. I then upgraded to a flip camera which is no longer made any more and then finally my most recent purchase was a Canon G20 and you can tell the difference is huge.

For you I would suggest you buy a cheap camera and start saving your BOR money until you can purchase a great camera with it. If done properly this will pay for itself over and over and over! The top thing to look for to me is the ability to record it in really low light because generally on stage or in a bar the light will suck chickens.

- **Hypnosis products**

CDs and DVDs of hypnosis sessions are a great money maker as well. Recording them is easy, buy borrow or rent a decent microphone that will plug and your laptop and record using either audacity or garage band. Add some soothing royalty-free music in the background, upload it to kunaki (A CD and DVD publishing service look it up its awesome) and order copies to have on hand.

For my CDs that is exactly what I did. For my DVDs I recorded the same type of stuff with my camera in front of my fireplace at home and they turned out looking pretty damn good. No its not a studio but if you go to some of the top guru's in self help it is almost exactely what they did starting out. Look up information on Brendan buchard if you don't believe me.

CD's and DVD's that I sell have 20 minute sessions and the same induction on each one. Why record again and again. Then they have patter directed at the problem and you are then golden.

These are all now offered as a digital download as well from my product website and are really just another proof point that I can do what I can say I can do on stage. I currently have something like 26 products available online!

The top products I found to sell as BOR are stop smoking, weight loss, stress management, insomnia and pain control.

- **Hypnosis Seminars**

A secondary way to generate income from shows especially public shows is to do a hypnosis seminar in the same venue or in a nearby venue the day after your show. Then during your show you mentioned that your holding at seminar the next day for weight loss or stress or stopping smoking, and you sell tickets to it. This is not something that I've currently been doing but in the past I have done very well at it. I would suggest charging a decent ticket price as your success rate will go up according to how much people spent.

Chapter 14 OK you a show booked it now it's time to promote!

Okay so you are booked into a public venue and now you have to promote the darn thing! You want it to be s success right! Don't depend on the person who booked you to do a dam thing! A great resource on how to promote a show is soldoutrun.com it has a lot and I do mean a lot of free information on how to promote a theater show and ours is no different! Well this is how I promote my events and generally it has worked out fairly well.

The 6 Week Show marketing plan

6 weeks out – Create and start to implement your marketing plan

Week 1: Creation of the next 6 weeks!

1. Grab your calendar and input all of this stuff
2. MONDAY Create promotional materials for event: Posters, Graphics, Facebook Event, Press releases, Photographs, and other stuff. (you may be able to use some of this stuff again and again.
3. Tuesday: Put posters up and make first post on face-book
4. Wednesday: Send out press releases to local media
5. Thursday: Book another show elsewhere
6. Friday: book another show elsewhere

Week 2

1. Monday: Create video interview about the show
2. Tuesday: Create venue highlight video
3. Wednesday: Put up Facebook Graphic about the show
4. Thursday: Look for other promotional partners

5. Friday: Look for other promotional partners

Week 3

1. Send out press release # 2
2. Put up Facebook interview video about the show
3. Wednesday: Book another show elsewhere
4. Thursday: Book another show elsewhere
5. Friday: Check and put up more posters

Week 4

1. Monday: Go book another show somewhere else
2. Tuesday: Send more press releases and give media outlets a call to make sure they are getting them
3. Wednesday: Put out Facebook video about the show
4. Thursday: Put out Facebook graphic about the show
5. Friday: Go to businesses to see if they would like to buy a table of tickets to the show and fill those seats!

Week 5

1. Monday: Go to more businesses and sell those seats
2. Tuesday: More press releases
3. Wednesday: Promote someone elses show
4. Face book venue highlight video
5. Facebook video why you are doing the show or video clip of what people can expect

Week 6

1. Monday: Facebook post and another press release
2. Tuesday: Facebook post
3. Wednesday: Sell tickets to the show, and Facebook post
4. Thursday: Sell tickets to local businesses
5. Friday: Sell tickets to local businesses

6. DO THE SHOW

You can tell by this plan you need to be a bloody salesman as well. When selling table tickets I generally go into local businesses and sell a full table of tickets for a discounted price. It helps bring people in and that is what you want to do! Of course please keep in mind all of this stuff changes over time so please be aware of how you plan to market your events and create your own system. Just because it has worked for me does not mean it will work for you!

Chapter 15: Problems on stage and how to handle them

We are winding down to the end of this book very quickly and I find it kind of sad, this book has taken a lot longer to write than I ever thought it would. I have poured my passion for hypnosis and the business into every page and with that of course comes its own problems. Speaking of problems not everything on stage is as rosy as it may sometimes appear. There will always be issues some you can ignore others you must deal with and that is really what this chapter is about. So let's go over how I deal with some of the common problems I find during shows.

- **Noise**

there is this huge myth that everything must be silent for a person to be hypnotized. This is completely false, when the room is very noisy I use what's called the sound around your patter, basically I just tell my volunteers that as they hear the sounds around them though sounds just allow them to go deeper and deeper relaxed further into that wonderful hypnotic state. That is really all you have to do, you may have to repeat it, or point out a specific sound like the phone ringing or a child crying depending on the situation.

- **Medical situations**

Medical situations can be a tough one, but its your job to keep control of the crowd and relax every one. I've had to medical situations come up during my shows in all of the years I have been performing.

The first situation was in my audience a lady passed out during the show, (her son was on stage and she laughed so hard and deeply that she passed out). While on stage during my final skit, I heard a cry from the audience we need a Doctor. To which I immediately responded "everyone on stage close your eyes and go deeper would a doctor please attend to the situation." I kept everyone on stage under control and let the doctor handle his work. The lady woke up within about a minute and a half and I finished the show.

My second medical situation happened just before I was about to go on at a graduation party. My sound person had just given the three minute warning that my show is about to start. The graduate class had rented bounce houses casino tables sumo suits and other fun stuff to do. Two girls were going on one final round of the sumo suits directly beside my stage. One girl pushed the other girl into the wall and hit her head so hard that it knocked her out. Thankfully one of the parents was a doctor in the audience. To keep the crowd of kids under control I grabbed my microphone and created a barrier between the doctor some of the students who were helping the girl and the actual audience. This allowed the helpers to do their job properly and kept the gawkers at bay.

Those are the type of things that can happen in your audience, but there's also something called an abreaction and if I have not covered it before it is when a person has a really odd reaction to hypnosis. There are several types and generally you can tell just by looking at you volunteers if something is wrong. The thing you need to remember if someone's having an abreaction is to remain calm and not touch them.

If I've said this before it's worth repeating during this part of the book. What you do is you say. "As you allow the scene to fade you can now attend to your breathing". And you repeat this again and again if necessary.

Abreactions can be useful if you are a hypnotherapist. However if you are not don't mess with people's heads just follow directions and say as you allow the scene to fade you can now attend to your breathing. That's it, they will generally calm down I've never seen one not, and then you simply dismiss them from your stage. You do not want a crazy nut up there with problems that you are not prepared to handle. This may sound mean but you are an entertainer not a psychotherapist not a counsellor a bloody entertainer and its your job to entertain.

So remember "the scene fades, and you attend to your breathing"

- No one goes under

What if nobody goes under? Is the show over? Probably but maybe not. This happened to me once early in my career and what I did then was redo my Pre-talk a little bit more in depth and a call for more volunteers. It worked! What I would do today would be a little different, in this book you've been given a whack of pre-tests which work almost automatically, so I would do two or three of those with the whole audience. Once I was done that I would call for volunteers again.

I could blame my subjects that night for not going under but the truth is it was me and my skills as a hypnotist. Know what you can and cannot do is important practice and be ready for anything.

- Crazy religious nuts

I love crazy people, I've had people with signs, I've had people interrupt my show, and I've had people interrupt my BOR sales, all saying that I'm going to hell- and chances are they're probably right.

However it's my right to perform my hypnosis show until the law says otherwise and in some areas it does. I would suggest to you that you never argue with somebody who is overly religious because you won't win. Simply state thank you for your opinion have a wonderful day. And if they continue on say thank you for your opinion have a wonderful day. And if they continue on say thank you for your opinion have a wonderful day.

It's much like a police officer be polite and courteous and you won't have a problem any bigger than the one you already have. If they are persistent, and really will not leave you alone, ask the people who hired you to be there and ask for them to be removed.

- Falling on the ground

a pet peeve of mine is hypnotists who lay people down on their stages. It may look dramatic it may make the hypnotist feel powerful but to me it's disrespectful to your volunteers. Would you like your wife or child laid on the ground or on the stage? You don't know what's on that stage whether the other volunteers of stepped in dog shit, or some other thing before the show. And some hypnotists actually encourage people falling out of the chair's and laying on the ground.

At a recent show I had this happen the man kept falling out of his chair and I knew had been have ties at least three times before by the same hypnotist. What I did was have him imagine a seat belt around him. I also got all of the other volunteers to do to because this can have a cascading effect where one volunteer falls out of their chair and then others do as well. By having them imagine a seatbelt and that they were belted into their chair it prevented them from falling out. I also give the warning that if they continue to fall out of their chair that they would not be allowed on my stage. This will stop 95% of all falling from chairs. If it continues I would suggest that you kick them back out into audience as it is your stage and your show and you are responsible for their safety.

- Disruptive volunteers

yes you will get ass hole volunteers, the ones it won't shut up the ones that won't quit moving and other crap too. The first step is to separate anyone who is sitting beside their friends and move them. If you see two people talking to each other when you call for volunteers than I would suggest that you move one to another section of the stage. If they continue to disrupt the other volunteers kick them back out into the audience. Your job will be more about keeping control on stage than anything else get rid of the jerks.

- **Continual laughter from volunteers**

often you will get people to come up and just giggle first separate them from your their friends and if that doesn't work use incorporation during your induction where if people hear laughter they will begin to laugh more and more and if the person is already laughing they find that it intensifies the more laughter they hear or produce. Then just simply get everyone to push that laughter away further and further until everyone is relaxed. I use this as a chance to incorporate what is happening on stage to induce hypnosis. This method has saved countless shows for me and allows me to get rid of the laughter without being a jerk.

- **Disruptive audience**

so let's say you are getting heckled by an audience member there really are only three things you can do.

1. Ignore it and hope it goes away generally it will.

By ignoring it the Heckler will lose the power that he thinks they have over you in general.

2. Acknowledge the heckling and engage in making the Heckler the centre of attention.

This is a dangerous path as if you do acknowledge it the Heckler does become the centre of attention and then does have power so if you are going to acknowledge it I would suggest that you stop the show and say I will not continue until that person calms down. This gets the audience on your side as you will not allow one person to ruin the whole show. However you must be careful depending on your audience type as the Heckler could be an important person in that audience for instance they could be a manager within the corporate audience you are performing for.

3. Acknowledge the Heckler and destroy them.
These is not recommended by me unless you have been on stage for years and know how to do it properly without coming off as a complete and total jerk.
I will generally not even engage the Heckler unless they are a real nuisance in which case I will actually ask for them to be removed. This is your show and it is not your job to deal with an ass hole. Sometimes it can actually be the booker who is your Heckler in which case I suggest you ignore it.

- No one volunteers

What if no one volunteers? You continue your Pre-talk and do some pre-tests with the whole audience. This allows them the opportunity to experience hypnosis and as you know once they've experienced it chances are they will be more willing to go into it. With the number of pre-tests you have in this book you can actually perform a full one hour walk around hypnosis show without being on stage at all just doing pre-tests.

- Bad introduction

this is a pet peeve of mine, which is why you're doing the exercise to create your introduction earlier in the book. I would suggest to you that you do create your introduction have a recorded on fiverr and use the damn thing. If a person is insisting on introducing you have your introduction laminated with you. Tell them it must be read word for word with no deviation as it's a very important part of the show.

- Pre-selected volunteers

most often this will happen at schools and I suggest you avoided if possible. What happens if the volunteers are preselected is that some of them may not actually want to be there. Do your normal pre-talk, let them know what is going to happen, and then do your hypnosis show. It will work out however you may need to do a longer induction or a longer Pre-talk.

- Quiet audiences

this is only a problem for some hypnotists that like a lot of noise like me. I do a lot of having audience shout out,, clap along, and doing actions during the show. For me I want them to feel as if they have went on a roller coaster and they are exhausted after the show. In a good way of course. So during my show I will have several instances where I ask them to be louder. In fact sometimes during my show I will get them to shout the trigger word and then complain that it wasn't loud enough and get them to do it again. This gets them engaged and active which is what I want during my show. For me my show is full audience participation not just the volunteers that come up.

Exercise:

I would like you to think up 10 other problems you think might happen on stage. Then I would like you to describe how you would solve them when they come up. This will give you a strong foundation in how you will deal with many of the different things that can happen as any type of performer.

1.

How to deal with it:

2.

How to deal with it:

3.

How to deal with it:

4.

How to deal with it:

5.

How to deal with it:

6.

How to deal with it:

7.

How to deal with it:

8.

How to deal with it:

9.

How to deal with it:

10.

How to deal with it:

Chapter 16 the final chapter (spoken in a very dramatic voice)

We have come to the final chapter, in this chapter I'm going to wrap everything up. We're going to cover adding emotion to your show, the different types of hypnosis shows you can have, hypnosis into the future my perspective, and quick start tips to get you on your way. Let's begin with adding emotion to your show.

Adding emotion to your show

There is no better way to get an audience hooked on your show then adding real relevant emotion from you as a performer to it. Think about all of the great performances you've ever seen. They all do one thing and that is get you emotionally hooked. So when you are dreaming up your skits and your show the number one bit of advice that I give you is to put yourself in to it.

Don't copy my show don't copy the greatest hypnotist you ever seen create your own show. Something you can be proud of something that holds your spirit within it.

This will create for you a show that is suited to you and makes a great difference. The people that it connects with will become your raving fans and absolutely book you again and again.

Other types of shows

This book has mainly focused on the comedy hypnosis show however there are a few other types of hypnosis show out there.

1. The motivational hypnosis show

This is the type of show that actually perform and while it has a lot of comedy there's also a lot of motivation involved to. When I created my motivational hypnosis show I thought through the skits so that at least four had a motivational connotation during the show. I could either exploit these motivational connotations during the skit itself or just after the skit. Along with my patented dreams coming true skit at the end of the show this creates in my opinion the best motivational hypnosis show on the market today. It also incorporates some of my story personal triumphs and losses and my life. It's something I'm extremely proud of and I know you to would be proud of yourself if you create a show that helped motivate and educate people as well. If you want dreams coming true look it up over on the stagehypnosiscenter.com

2. The metaphysical show

Some people do still believe that hypnosis has some weird metaphysical connotation and if you choose to go this route you can look at some of the great spiritism shows of the past and even the psychic shows of today, hypnosis fits really well into this type of show however it's just not for me.

If you are mentalist or a psychic entertainer this may be the route you choose to go with hypnosis. Performing everything from séance's using hypnosis to old time spook shows is possible. As long as you do it in an ethical manner I believe it's perfectly fine.

Hypnosis into the future

The one thing that hypnosis has to do to jump up to the level of other forms of art is to get a hit television show. Hypnosis has never ever had one. A hit television show would do two things to the hypnosis industry first it would allow us to hypnotize people easier second it would bring a bunch of new blood good or bad into the hypnosis world. For too long hypnosis has been an old boys club where only a select few were taught the skills to do hypnosis shows. In recent years it's become a prostitute for those who want to teach it but have never really performed on stage. The fact is hypnosis is extremely easy to do if you have the guts to do it.

When you are performing I would like you to think about what you believe should be the future of hypnosis and then please go in that direction. All of our futures could depend on you so be safe on stage, elevate the art of hypnosis because that's what it is an art, and be very careful with the future of this industry.

Your quick start tips

This is the final section and there is only one thing that I will tell you is a quick start tip and that is to get off your ass and go perform some hypnosis, you might fail 100 times, I don't care go do it for hundred more and then 100 more after that and then you might start getting results.

You did not learn to read and write in one day it probably took you a year or so to be able to do that. Hypnosis can be just as intricate as reading and writing so give it the attention it deserves. Book your first show and before you do it book 10 more. Before those 10 are complete book 20 more. Before those 20 are complete book 100 more.

After you've got through your first 100 shows see what you've done. Those first 100 shows may take you two years it did for me. Or you might do 100 shows in three months it all depends on you. Go out there and live your dreams!

Now go out there and hypnotized people!

Thank you from the bottom of my heart

Jesse

Jesse Lewis hypnosis

Made in the USA
San Bernardino, CA
15 December 2019